BRIDGE

CONVENTIONS

FINESSES AND COUPS

Terence Reese

Dover Publications, Inc.

New York

Published in Canada by General Publishing Company, Ltd., 30 Lesmill Road, Don Mills, Toronto, Ontario.
Published in the United Kingdom by Constable and Company, Ltd., 10 Orange Street, London WC 2.

This Dover edition, first published in 1970, is an unabridged and unaltered republication of the work originally published in 1965. It is reprinted by special arrangement with Sterling Publishing Company, Inc., 419 Park Avenue South, New York City 10016, publisher of the original, "Cornerstone Library," edition.

International Standard Book Number: 0-486-22631-X
Library of Congress Catalog Card Number: 76-116819

Manufactured in the United States of America
Dover Publications, Inc.
180 Varick Street
New York, N.Y. 10014

FOREWORD

This book is derived from, but is far more than a new edition of, *The Bridge Player's Dictionary* which was published six years ago. Elementary definitions and sections relating to laws and penalties have been omitted. Added are accounts of many new conventions and every title has been redrafted in the light of contemporary practice.

In particular, every convention that is permitted in American tournaments is described—every convention, that is, whose nature is not self-evident from the title. As explained under *Conventions*, the American Contract Bridge League lists some conventions as permissible in all tournaments (Class 1), some as optional with the tournament committee (Class 2), and some as permissible only in special events (Class 2A). Thought was given to noting these distinctions in the text, but the decision went against including such classifications as they are subject to constant review and change. The ACBL authorities tend to give all new ideas a probationary spell in Class 2, whether they create a problem for opponents or not.

Another reason for not tying to the ACBL classification is that this would have meant excluding a number of conventions of undoubted merit that have not so far been officially recognized.

In the field of play the title has been stretched to include not only finesses and coups, but many other tactical moves.

The aim is to make this a tournament player's handbook. It does not set out to rival the Official Encyclopedia, but perhaps it will be regarded as the quintessence of the practical side of that great work.

Albert Dormer has collaborated with me at every stage in the preparation of this volume and its predecessor. His experience on the editorial staff of the ACBL *Bulletin* has been invaluable.

TERENCE REESE

ACES OVER TWO-BIDS

In some systems the responder to a strong two-bid is required to show aces immediately. In response to an artificial two clubs, for example, partner bids two diamonds if he has no ace. With one ace, he bids the suit in which the ace is held (three diamonds to show the ace of diamonds). With two aces, he bids 3 NT. If he has no ace but 8 or more points, including two kings, he responds 2 NT.

For a special treatment, see *Schenken System* (two-diamond opening).

ACOL SYSTEM

This system is played by the majority of British players and its general philosophy is shared by leading West Coast players. Some of its ideas are reflected in modern American systems such as Stayman and Kaplan-Sheinwold.

1. **Opening suit bids of one** range from tactical, semi-psychic bids on as little as $1\frac{1}{2}$ or 2 honor-tricks, up to hands of $5\frac{1}{2}$ honor-tricks that are not of game-going strength. (Acol players use point-count only for no-trump bidding.) As will be seen below, Acol has more sign-off bids than most systems and in general the bidding can stop more readily than in other forms of approach bidding. This provides a safety factor for opening bids that are under strength in high cards but possess a good trump suit.

2. **Opening 1 NT** is variable: according to the book, 12 to 14 points not vulnerable, 16 to 18 vulnerable.

A simple take-out of 1 NT into two of a suit is discouraging. The Stayman convention is used on hands that present a choice of final contract.

3. **The Acol two-bid,** two spades, two hearts, or two diamonds, shows a hand of "power and quality" and is forcing for one round. A strong hand containing not less than 8 playing tricks is usually worth a two-bid:

     ♠ A K Q J 6 3   ♡ A 7 4   ◇ A 8 5   ♣ 6

     ♠ 7   ♡ A K Q 10 4   ◇ K Q J 6 5   ♣ A 8

Those are characteristic two-openings, but the bid may also be made on hands of good honor strength and slightly less playing strength. For example:

♠ A K J 10 5   ♡ A 6 2   ◇ K Q 4 3   ♣ A

The weakness response to an Acol two-bid is 2 NT.

Any other response shows at least one honor-trick. A double raise of an Acol two shows good values with no ace or void.

4. **The Acol two-club bid** guarantees a minimum of 5 honor-tricks and is forcing to game except when the opener rebids 2 NT over the weakness response of two diamonds.

For a positive response, there are no strict requirements. In general, about one honor-trick for a response at the level of two, 1½ honor-tricks when a suit (clubs or diamonds) has to be bid at the range of three.

5. **Opening bids of three** are pre-emptive, as in standard bidding.

6. **The Culbertson 4-5 NT** is recommended for slam bidding.

Among tournament players, the following conventions are assumed to be part of Acol: *Unusual No-Trump, Responsive Double, Swiss Convention, Truscott Convention, Texas, Flint Convention, Fourth Suit Forcing.*

Historically, the Acol system began as a reaction against the early approach-forcing style in which the bidding was developed with excessive slowness. One of the early Acol sayings was, "You bid what you think you can make and you pass when you feel like it."

Many bids that would be forcing in Standard American are limit-bids or sign-offs in Acol. In response to an opening bid of one, 2 NT is a natural value call showing about 11 to 12 points. A rebid of his own suit over 2 NT, either by opener or responder, is discouraging. A double raise, even in a major, is non-forcing.

ADVANCE CUE-BID

A player makes an advance cue-bid when he shows a side control before supporting his partner's suit. For example:

(See hand on next page.)

	South	North
	1♠	2◇
	3♡	?

North holds:

♠ 10 x   ♡ K 10 x x   ◇ K 10 x x x   ♣ A x

In the ordinary way, a trump suit has to be agreed on before a cue-bid can safely be made. But here, if North calls four hearts to agree on the suit, South may pass and a slam may be missed.

If North were to call five hearts instead of four hearts, that would describe his values more adequately but would not show specifically the first-round club control.

The solution lies in an advance cue-bid of four clubs over South's three hearts. On the next round North will clarify matters by calling hearts. So the bidding may go:

	South	North
	1♠	2◇
	3♡	4♣ (advance cue-bid)
	4◇ (natural)	5♡

Now it will be clear to South that four clubs was an advance cue-bid.

See also *Out of the Blue Cue-Bid* and *Void-Showing Bid*.

ADVANCE SACRIFICE

When a player is prepared to sacrifice at a certain level, it can be good tactics for him to call at that level before he has to. That is called an advance sacrifice. The intention is to crowd the auction and present the opponents with a difficult decision. For example, with North-South vulnerable the bidding goes:

South	West	North	East
1◇	1♡	2♠	6♡

East holds:

♠ 10 x   ♡ K x x x x   ◇ x   ♣ J x x x

After West's overcall and North's forcing bid, East is prepared to sacrifice as high as six hearts. Rather than give North-South a chance to exchange information, East makes the advance sacrifice of six hearts, forcing the enemy to judge their next move at a high level.

ASKING-BIDS

Asking-bids are a conventional way of locating controls for slam purposes. They can be used to supplement a 4 NT convention, such as Blackwood, but in their original form are not compatible with cue-bidding.

According to the Culbertson method, a bid can be recognized as an asking bid when it is either:

(a) A bid in a new suit at the four-level or higher, following immediately upon the agreement of a trump suit.

(b) An unnecessary (or double) jump in a new suit at the three-level or higher. (An unnecessary jump is a bid one trick higher than is necessary for a jump-shift.)

South	North
1♠	3♠
4♦ (asking-bid)	

South	North
1♣	3♣
4♠ (asking-bid)	

South	North
1♠	2♣
4♣	4♠ (*not* an asking-bid)

South	North
1♦	3♠ (asking-bid)

In the last example diamonds are agreed by inference as the trump suit.

The responder to an asking-bid has to show his controls, which are defined as follows:

First-round control	—	ace or void
Second-round control	—	king or singleton
Third-round control	—	queen or doubleton

The response to an asking-bid depends on two features: the controls held in the "asked" suit, and the controls held in other suits.

Responses to the first asking-bid

Controls in asked suit	Controls in other suits	Response
No first- or second-round	Immaterial	Sign off in agreed trump suit
Second-round	No first-round	Sign off in agreed trump suit
Second-round	One first-round	Bid the first-round control. (With trump ace, jump one trick)
First-round	No first-round	Raise asked suit
Second-round	2 aces (not voids)	Bid 4 NT
Ace (not void)	1 ace (not void)	Bid 4 NT
Second-round	3 aces (not voids)	Bid 5 NT
Ace (not void)	2 aces (not voids)	Bid 5 NT

Where the responder has the requirements for a 4 NT response and a void in an outside suit, he may jump in the suit of the void.

There are also ways of making repeat asking-bids in the same suit or subsequent asking-bids in another suit.

Asking-bids are seldom played in America but in different forms are included in Italian and most other Continental systems.

See also *Trump Asking-Bids*.

ASTRO

This is the most complicated of the methods that have been devised for competing against an opponent's 1 NT opening. The name is derived from the initial letters of the inventors, Allinger, Stern and Rosler.

In principle, an overcall of *two clubs* over 1 NT (either by second hand or by fourth hand after two passes) indicates a two-suiter containing *hearts* and a minor suit. An overcall of *two diamonds* indicates *spades* and another suit.

South opens 1 NT and West, not vulnerable, holds:

♠ K Q 8 4 2   ♡ 7   ◇ K 10 4   ♣ A Q J 8

If not playing any special convention, it would be dangerous for West either to double or bid two spades. Playing Astro he can make the conventional overcall of two diamonds with a good chance of landing on his feet.

The responder to the Astro overcall acts as follows:

1. With three-card or longer support for the "anchor" major (spades in the example above), he bids this suit at an appropriate level.

2. With a good hand, containing some support for the anchor major, he bids 2 NT, forcing for one round.

3. With length in the artificial suit (two clubs or two diamonds), he may pass or raise.

4. With an independent six-card suit of his own, he may bid that suit.

5. Lacking any of these features, he bids the intermediate suit, two hearts over two diamonds, or two diamonds over two clubs. This is called a "neutral" response. (Continental players would call it a "relay.")

After the neutral response the Astro bidder may either:

1. Bid the anchor suit when he has at least five cards. (If he dislikes the anchor suit, responder may then bid 2 NT, asking for the second suit.)

2. Bid his second suit at the three level. To follow this sequence, the Astro bidder will generally need a six-card minor suit.

3. Pass the neutral response when this is his second suit. Or

4. Bid 2 NT, constructive and asking for further information.

A jump to three of any suit over 1 NT is pre-emptive. With a strong two-suiter the Astro player overcalls with 2 NT.

The Astro method provides more defensive opportunities than similar systems such as *Landy* or *Ripstra*, but is more difficult to handle. The players must have an understanding about the meaning of a redouble in various sequences.

ASTRO CUE-BID

Immediate overcalls in the opponent's suit are underemployed in standard systems, and a suggestion from the "Astro" stable is that they be used to denote a special class of two-suiter, where the minor suit is longer than the major. The overcall shows clubs and hearts, unless one of those suits has been bid. In that case, two clubs over one club indicates diamonds and hearts, two hearts over one heart indicates clubs and spades.

When not vulnerable, the cue-bid is mainly defensive in purpose.

When vulnerable, the strength will be equal to a sound vulnerable overcall in the minor suit, with the added information of length in a major.

♠ 9   ♥ A J 7 4 2   ♦ 6   ♣ Q J 10 8 4 2

Not vulnerable, overcall one spade with two spades.

♠ 5   ♥ A Q 10 4   ♦ A Q J 9 6 2   ♣ 5 3

Vulnerable, overcall one club with two clubs.
Compare *Colorful Cue-bid* and *Michaels Cue-bid*.

AUTOMATIC SQUEEZE

A squeeze is said to be automatic, as opposed to simple (or one-way), when it would be equally effective against either defender: the discard from dummy does not depend on the play of the left-hand opponent. The following illustrates the difference between an automatic squeeze and a simple squeeze.

First, an example of a simple squeeze:

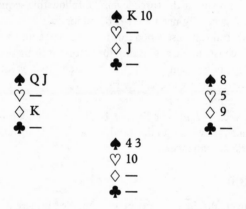

Playing at no trump, South cashes the ten of hearts and squeezes West. That is a one-way squeeze. It works only when West holds the key cards.

Now exchange the East-West cards and at the same time transfer the one-card threat from North to South:

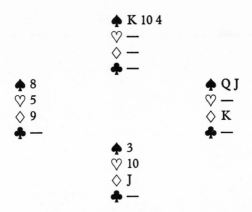

Now the squeeze is automatic and it works against either opponent. Technically, it may be expressed in this way:

In a simple (or one-way) squeeze the two-card threat and the one-card threat are in the same hand, opposite the squeeze card. The squeeze is effective only against the opponent who discards first.

In an automatic squeeze the one-card threat and the squeeze card are in the same hand, opposite the two-card threat. When the squeeze card is played, the discard from the opposite hand is automatic and does not depend on the left-hand opponent's discard.

AVOIDANCE PLAY

This name can be given to any tactical stroke that is aimed at keeping a particular defender out of the lead while the declarer establishes his tricks. The maneuver often takes place within the suit that is being established:

A K 8 3

Q 10 5   J 9 7

6 4 2

Suppose that declarer needs three tricks from this suit and cannot afford to let East gain the lead.

If the ace and king are laid down, West can thwart declarer by throwing the queen. The avoidance play is to lead twice from the South hand. If West plays low each time, dummy wins and West has

11

to take the third round of the suit. If, however, West seeks to unblock by playing the queen on the first or second round, dummy ducks and West is allowed to hold the trick.

At trump contracts avoidance play may be necessary to prepare the ground for ruffing:

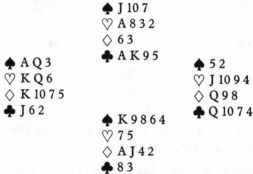

```
              ♠ J 10 7
              ♡ A 8 3 2
              ◇ 6 3
              ♣ A K 9 5
♠ A Q 3                      ♠ 5 2
♡ K Q 6                      ♡ J 10 9 4
◇ K 10 7 5                   ◇ Q 9 8
♣ J 6 2                      ♣ Q 10 7 4
              ♠ K 9 8 6 4
              ♡ 7 5
              ◇ A J 4 2
              ♣ 8 3
```

South plays in two spades after West has opened the bidding; West leads the king of hearts.

Expecting to lose two trump tricks, declarer can count only three tricks in trump and four top winners in the side suits. He therefore requires at least one diamond ruff. It is important to keep East out of the lead. Otherwise East may lead a trump and kill dummy's ruffs.

At trick one, therefore, the king of hearts is allowed to hold. This is the first avoidance play. If West continues a heart, dummy wins and leads a diamond. When East plays low, declarer inserts the jack. That is the second avoidance play.

In another type of avoidance play declarer switches his losers from one suit to another. He presents the harmless defender with an unexpected trick, so as to avoid losing a trick to the dangerous player:

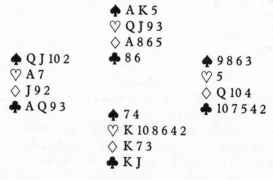

```
              ♠ A K 5
              ♡ Q J 9 3
              ◇ A 8 6 5
♠ Q J 10 2    ♣ 8 6         ♠ 9 8 6 3
♡ A 7                        ♡ 5
◇ J 9 2                      ◇ Q 10 4
♣ A Q 9 3                    ♣ 10 7 5 4 2
              ♠ 7 4
              ♡ K 10 8 6 4 2
              ◇ K 7 3
              ♣ K J
```

West opens one club, North doubles and South eventually plays in four hearts. The queen of spades is led.

Declarer's main hope is for a three-three diamond break, so that he can throw a club on dummy's fourth diamond. East, meanwhile, must not be allowed in to lead a club.

To prevent East from gaining the lead in diamonds, dummy plays low on the opening lead and South later discards a diamond on the third round of spades. Then he establishes dummy's fourth diamond by ruffing, East having had no opportunity to lead a club.

For another kind of avoidance play, see *Scissors Coup*.

BACKWARD FINESSE

In some situations where a natural finesse would fail, the enemy honor can be picked up by a finesse taken in the opposite direction.

K x x

Q x x   10 x x x

A J 9

A simple finesse of the jack would lose to the queen. Possession of the nine, however, enables South to execute a backward finesse. He can lead the jack and, if this is covered by the queen, he can finesse the nine on the way back.

A backward finesse, as compared with a simple finesse, depends for success on two cards being favorably placed: in the example above, the queen and the ten. The maneuver is accordingly more common in defense, when a player can see from the dummy that a natural finesse would lose:

9 x x

Q x x   K 10 8 x

A J x

A declarer playing this combination from the West position would normally finesse East's ten. But if East were defending and had the lead he would initiate a backward finesse by leading the ten.

BARON SYSTEM

This British system was developed in the 1940's, primarily by Leo Baron and Adam Meredith. Nowadays it is seldom played in its entirety, but the Baron group was ahead of its time and pioneered many techniques that are an accepted part of modern systems. Among these were a weak no-trump throughout, inverted minor suit raises, exaggerated "balancing," 2 NT over 1 NT forcing, Baron grand slam try (see *Grand Slam Force*), delayed game raises, and fourth suit forcing.

BATH COUP

This is a simple hold-up play by declarer when he holds A J x and the king is led:

x x x

K Q 10 x   x x x

A J x

Having let the king hold the first trick, South has a major tenace and will win two tricks if West continues the suit.

The same strategical play can be made when the ace and jack are in different hands:

A x x

K Q 10 x   x x x

J x x

By holding up when the king is led, South makes it impractical for West to continue.

When the ace is held by South and the guarded jack by dummy, South can win two tricks by force and will usually capture the king.

BIDDABLE SUITS

Some systems lay down certain standards for biddable suits. In general American practice any five-card suit can be opened, or any four-card suit as good as A 10 x x or Q J x x. A weaker four-card suit can be opened if the hand contains another near-biddable suit.

Modern American systems for the most part require five cards for a major-suit opening and allow minor-suit openings on three-card suits.

In responding to partner's bid, there is less emphasis on the need for a biddable suit. It is commonplace to bid weak suits when no better choice can be found. A suit take-out by a passed hand, however, is generally made in a playable suit.

For opening bids on a three-card club suit, see *Short Club*.

BIG CLUB

See *Schenken System*.

BLACKWOOD CONVENTION

In this popular convention, originated by Easley Blackwood of Indianapolis, a bid of 4 NT, other than a quantitative 4 NT, asks partner to show his total number of aces in accordance with a step system:

Five clubs shows no ace
Five diamonds shows one ace
Five hearts shows two aces
Five spades shows three aces

Holding all four aces, the response is again five clubs. There should be no ambiguity, for two players holding no aces between them would hardly be looking for a slam.

If the 4 NT bidder calls 5 NT over his partner's response, that announces that all four aces are held in the combined hands and asks for kings to be shown. Six clubs shows no kings, six diamonds shows one king, and so on.

Void suits

These are not counted as aces in responding to Blackwood. However, there is a way of showing a void provided the general strength of the hand warrants strong action. The responder to 4 NT bids the suit which

15

shows the appropriate number of aces at the six-level. For example, with two aces and a void he would respond six hearts instead of five hearts, if he felt his hand were good enough.

Five no-trump to play

When the response to 4 NT is unsatisfactory for slam purposes, the Blackwood bidder will sometimes wish to call a halt in 5 NT. He cannot call 5 NT over his partner's response to 4 NT, for that would ask for kings. Instead, he calls five in any unbid suit: that requires his partner to call 5 NT, which can be passed. For example:

South	North
—	1♡
2◇	4◇
4 NT	5♡
5♠	5 NT
Pass	

South decides that a slam should not be bid, but he is already past the five diamond level. As 5 NT may still be safe, he calls an unbid suit over his partner's response to Blackwood. Over South's five spades, North is obliged to call 5 NT and South passes.

When opponents interfere

The responder to Blackwood is not compelled to show his aces if the opponents make a bid over 4 NT, but he may do so if he wishes. In that event, he responds by steps starting from the opponent's bid. For example:

South	West	North	East
1♡	4◇	4♡	Pass
4 NT	5◇	?	

If North bid five hearts, that would promise one ace. Five spades would promise two aces, and so on. A pass would mean either that North had no ace or that he was not prepared to show one. A double by North would be a penalty double.

See also *Four-Club Blackwood, Gerber Convention, Roman Blackwood,* and *Super Blackwood.*

BLOCKING PLAY

This is a play that causes the run of an enemy suit to be blocked. There is often occasion for a blocking play on the opening lead, as in this well-known position:

A 7

K J 8 5 2   Q 6

10 9 4 3

West leads the five against a no-trump contract. If dummy plays low, East will win and return the suit, and when West gets in he will run three more tricks.

By going up with dummy's ace on the opening lead, South can prevent the run of the suit when the enemy regains the lead. The play will be especially effective if West has only one entry and that can be attacked at once.

In the example above, the blocking play can hardly be wrong, for West is most unlikely to have led a low card from K Q J x x.

In the next example declarer has to read the distribution accurately:

8 4

Q 7 2   A 10 6 5 3

K J 9

Suppose that East has bid this suit and South eventually plays in no trump. West leads the two, the ace is put up and the five returned. Playing West for three to the queen, declarer refuses the finesse and puts up the king to block the suit. This, of course, would be a "wrong view" if West had led from 10 x x.

Good card reading is required in the following position:

(See hand on next page.)

K 8 7 5 3 2

J 10 4   A 9

Q 6

At no trump, with the lead in dummy, declarer has only one outside entry to the table. When dummy leads small, East must go up with the ace and immediately knock out dummy's entry.

The play of a high card to prevent declarer from gaining an entry is also a form of blocking play:

Q x x x

A x x   J 10 x x

K x

Suppose that South leads low with the object of entering the North hand. By going up with the ace, West can block the entry. The next is a more advanced example of the same type of play:

Q 9 x

A 10 x x   K x x

J x x

Declarer leads small, intending to finesse the nine. He cannot be prevented from establishing a trick in the suit, but he can be denied entry to dummy. West must insert the ten, covered by the queen and king, and on the next round West can play his ace if South leads low.

BLUFF NO-TRUMP OVERCALL

See *Gardener No-Trump Overcall.*

BULLDOG SYSTEM

This was one of the first systems to break away from traditional American patterns and introduce some radical ideas. It was developed principally by William Hanna and Douglas Steen. Among its features are weak two-bids, controlled psychics, five-card majors, and weak jump-shift responses.

Four-card majors are seldom opened unless the suit is very strong. A three-card minor may be bid instead.

1 NT opening varies according to vulnerability: 17 to 19 points when vulnerable; 12 to 14 points when not vulnerable.

Jump-shift responses are pre-emptive and are based on a six-card or longer suit with few points. The only exception is a jump-shift response of three clubs, which is forcing (see below).

Psychic opening bids may be made on 7 points or less. They are usually based on a four-card or longer suit containing at least a queen. Psychic bids are seldom made when vulnerable.

A player who has opened with a psychic bid must pass any response other than three clubs or 2 NT.

Three clubs response to suit opening is conventional and forcing. It promises sufficient strength to play at the three-level, opposite even a minimum psychic opening.

Opener must respond three diamonds if his opening bid was a psychic. Any rebid other than three diamonds shows that the opening was genuine.

2 NT response to suit opening shows about 20 to 23 points. If the opening bid was a psychic, opener now bids the full value of his hand. Thus, if he had psyched with a balanced seven-point hand he would raise 2 NT to 3 NT. If he had psyched on a worthless hand he would pass. If he had a good suit he might jump to game in that suit.

To show a legitimate opening after the 2 NT response, the opener bids three in a new suit.

Weak two-bids are used, with two clubs the only forcing opening. Weak jump overcalls are also played.

Other conventions

A number of special conventions are incorporated, some of which can be used apart from the Bulldog system. The following come into this category and are described separately:

Kivi Convention, Miles Convention, Okuneff Convention and *Responsive Double.*

The Bulldog system also uses an elaborate code of asking-bids for slam purposes, called Rush asking-bids after Courtland Rush, one of their originators.

CANAPÉ

This is the name for the French style of bidding in which short biddable suits are called before long ones. For example:

♠ A Q 10 x x x   ♡ K x   ◇ K Q x x   ♣ x

The opening bid on this hand is one diamond. When spades are shown on the next round, partner knows that the spades are longer than the diamonds.

The same principle applies when the shorter suit is the higher ranking. Thus, when an opening bid of one spade is followed by two hearts on the second round, that shows that the hearts are at least as long as the spades and may be longer.

The Canapé method is also followed in some of the Italian systems. It will be noted that in many sequences it enables the players to exchange extra information without raising the level of the bidding.

CHEAPER MINOR

See *Lower Minor Convention.*

COLORFUL CUE-BID

An immediate overcall of an opponent's major-suit opening to show a limited major-minor two-suiter. The suits are always of the same color. Thus, two spades over one spade shows the red suits, two hearts over one heart the black suits. The convention was devised by Mrs. Dorothy Hayden of Hastings-on-Hudson, N.Y., and is played by her with B. Jay Becker.

COMBINATION FINESSE

A combination finesse is played when two cards of equal rank are missing and the declarer may have to finesse a second time:

$$A \ J \ 10$$

$$x \ x \ x$$

South leads low and finesses the ten. If that loses to the king or queen, he later takes a second finesse against the outstanding honor.

$$A \ J \ 9$$

$$x \ x \ x$$

The best chance to win two tricks is to begin with a deep finesse of the nine. If that draws the king or queen, there will be a simple finesse for the remaining high honor.

$$K \ 10 \ 9 \ x$$

$$x \ x \ x$$

After a first-round finesse of the nine has fetched the jack or queen, the ten is finessed on the next round.

See also *Double Finesse.*

CONTROLLED PSYCHICS

A controlled psychic, as opposed to an ordinary psychic, is one made in accordance with a prearranged system (which should, of course, be made known to the opponents) and protected from danger by the operation of signals and hand-brakes.

Such bids generally take the form of an opening bid on a near-worthless hand. The player passes on the next round except when his partner shows a very powerful hand; then some special devices come into operation.

Systems that feature controlled psychics include Bulldog, Kaplan-Sheinwold, Roth-Stone and Stayman. As an illustration, the provisions of the Stayman system for controlled psychics are outlined below. (The provisions of other systems are mentioned briefly under their respective titles.)

Psychic openings in the Stayman system

Psychic openings may be made by first or second hand when not vulnerable. The strength is in the 3- to 6-point range and the suit should be of five or six cards, preferably headed by a queen at least.

Rebid by a psychic opener

A psychic opener may pass any response except a jump-shift. (With 19 or more points, partner is obliged to make a jump-shift.)

After a jump-shift, opener must make a minimum rebid in no trump if his opening was psychic. Thus, the sequence one diamond—two hearts—2 NT shows that the opening bid was psychic.

If, after a jump-shift, opener announces a psychic by making a minimum rebid in no trump, the responder can pass or can make a non-forcing call in one of the partnership suits. If he wishes to force a further bid from his partner he must change the suit.

See also *Skinner Psychic Control.*

CONVENTIONS

The use of conventions in duplicate play is controlled by the ACBL (American Contract Bridge League). Most familiar conventions are listed as Class 1. These must be allowed in sectional games. Conventions listed by the ACBL as Class 2 are optional with the tournament committee or director. Those listed as Class 2A are allowed only in international trials or in team matches scored by total points or international match points.*

Departures from convention

It is never unethical for a player to depart from a convention that has been announced, so long as partner has no means, other than by the exercise of his judgment, of assessing what is happening. In a sentence: *"A convention in bidding is an agreement between partners, not an undertaking to the opponents."*

CO-OPERATIVE DOUBLE

There are some bidding situations in which a player makes a double that is, by definition, a penalty double, but does not expect his partner

* See *Foreword.*

to pass unless the double suits him well. A penalty double of that kind is said to be a co-operative double.

The following is an example of a double that would be understood to be co-operative:

Rubber bridge, both sides vulnerable and 60 on score:

South	West	North	East
1◇	Pass	1 NT	2♣
2◇	3♣	Pass	Pass
Double			

Clearly, South intends that North should use his discretion in deciding whether to pass the double of three clubs or call three diamonds. South's failure to double two clubs, and his free bid of two diamonds, have described his hand within reasonable limits and it is now up to North to make use of that information.

COUNTING THE HAND

A player is said to "count the hand" when he works out the exact distribution of the unseen hands. This is a regular process on the part of good players.

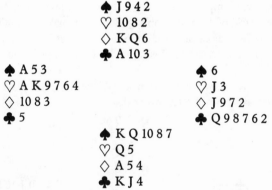

South plays in four spades after West has opened one heart. The defense begins with three rounds of hearts, East ruffs and South over-ruffs. When trumps are led West wins the second round and exits with his last trump.

Declarer needs to find the queen of clubs to make his contract. The correct technique is to try to obtain a count of the hand before playing clubs. After the third round of trumps declarer cashes the diamonds.

23

When West follows to three rounds he is known to have started with at least three diamonds, six hearts and three spades. He cannot, therefore, hold more than one club, so declarer can assure his contract by playing off dummy's ace of clubs and finessing against East.

COUP EN PASSANT

This is a trump coup combined with a loser-on-loser play. The term is based on the analogy of the pawn capture *en passant* at chess. This is an example:

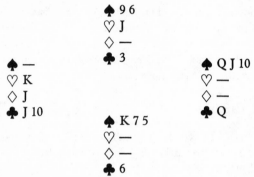

Spades are trump and South needs two of the last four tricks. Dummy leads the jack of hearts, enabling South to make a small trump *en passant*. If East discards his club, South ruffs; if East ruffs the jack of hearts, South discards his losing club. Either way, South takes two tricks.

The *coup en passant* is by no means rare in practical play. The above position arises from the following deal:

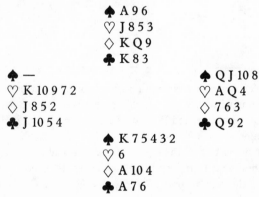

South plays in four spades and the defense begins with two rounds of hearts. Declarer ruffs and leads a trump to the ace. When the bad break is discovered, declarer's best chance is to ruff another heart and cash his top winners in the minor suits, finishing in dummy. So long as East has to follow suit, declarer will be certain to succeed, for he will reach the end position shown above.

COVERING HONORS

When an enemy card high is led for a finesse, it is generally right for second hand to cover, in accordance with the whist maxim, "Always cover an honor with an honor." For example:

J x

Q 9 x   K x x

A 10 8 x x

If dummy leads the jack, East should cover. Otherwise declarer can make four tricks.

Where the high card is led from a sequence of honors, however, the player should usually not cover until the last honor of the sequence is led:

Q J 9 x

10 x x   K x x

A x x

Dummy leads the queen. If East puts on the king declarer need not lose a trick, for on the second round he can finesse against West's ten. Following the rule, "Cover the last honor of a sequence," East would allow the queen to ride but he would cover the jack if that were led on the next round.

Nevertheless, with a doubleton king or queen it is usually better to cover touching honors, for otherwise the defender's card may die a useless death on the next round. For example:

J 10 3

A 9 7 6   Q 4

K 8 5 2

When dummy leads the jack, East should not hold back the queen. In such cases it is better to cover and hope that some lower card will be established in partner's hand.

When the high card comes from declarer, second hand will often have a difficult decision. One old rule is to cover when there are two honors on the left, but not when there is only one. For example:

A 10 8 6 3

Q 5 4   K 9 2

J 7

When South leads the jack, West does better to cover. On the other hand, if South had held K J 9 the cover would have been a mistake, saving the declarer a guess: that is the defender's dilemma.

In the next example there is only one honor on the defender's left and the cover cannot gain.

A 8 6 3

Q 5 4   K 9 2

J 10 7

On the first round the jack must be allowed to run to the king. If South follows with the ten later, then West will have to cover.

Since the object of covering an enemy honor is to promote lower cards in the hand of one or the other defender, it would be doubly foolish for West to cover in a situation such as the following:

A 10 9 8

K 6 4 3   Q 7 2

J 5

When South leads the jack, West can see that covering with the king will not help to promote any low card. Moreover, the king will control the fourth round of the suit if South has only a doubleton.

The defense is more difficult when the lead comes from dummy:

J 5

K 6 4 3

Now it will be wrong for East to cover the jack if South has a holding such as A Q 10 9 or A 10 9 8; but right to cover when South has A Q x or A Q x x.

CRASHING HONORS

There are a number of artful ways in which a declarer may induce the defenders to crash their high cards on one another. As was remarked under the previous title, *Covering Honors*, it is generally right for the second-hand player to cover the lead of an unsupported high card. Declarer can exploit that tendency in situations such as the following:

Q x x x

A   K x

J 10 9 x x x

Dummy leads the queen in the hope that East may cover.

More subtle examples of this kind of play occur when the declarer's honors are not in sequence:

$$Q x x x$$

$$10 x x x x$$

Suppose that declarer can judge that East has two or more cards in this suit. To lead dummy's Queen cannot cost and may provoke East, holding K J x or A J x, to cover, telescoping the defenders' tricks.

A defender who is marked with length in the trump suit can often be subjected to psychological pressure of that kind:

$$J x x$$

$$A \qquad\qquad K Q 9 x$$

$$10 8 x x x$$

If East is marked with length in the suit it may gain to lead the jack. East may cover, thinking that declarer has A 10 8 x x and that to duck would lose a tempo unnecessarily. The same is true of the following situation:

$$J x x x$$

$$Q \qquad\qquad K 10 8 x$$

$$A 9 7 x$$

In the above examples the declarer has to be able to infer that a particular defender has length in the suit. Otherwise, the honor-crashing play may cost a trick. For instance, in the last example the lead of the jack would be a losing play if East held a singleton.

There is another group of plays in which the attempt to crash honors is a "free shot" that cannot cost. For example:

J 7

K   Q 10 9 3

A 8 6 5 4 2

Dummy leads the jack and if East covers, the defenders can be held to two tricks instead of three.

In a final example, dummy leads a high card but declarer has no intention of letting it run:

9 x x x

A K Q 7 x

Provided there are plentiful entries to the table, to lead the nine is a subtlety that costs nothing. If East does not cover, declarer plays high. Once in a while, East will hold the outstanding four cards and may be persuaded to cover the nine. Then his high cards can be picked up by subsequent finesses.

CRISS-CROSS SQUEEZE

This is a squeeze that depends upon an unusual arrangement of divided threats. Declarer and dummy both have an isolated winning card, with two cards of lower rank lying opposite.

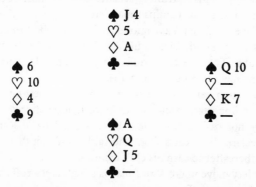

In this ending there is no two-card threat headed by a winner, such as exists in other forms of squeeze, but there is compensation in the form of extra entries. South leads the queen of hearts and East is squeezed. Whichever suit East unguards, declarer cashes the winner and crosses to the opposite hand to make the long card.

The criss-cross squeeze is always an automatic squeeze: it will work against either opponent so long as both guards are in the same hand.

CROSS-RUFF PLAY

A cross-ruff takes place when plain suits are ruffed alternately in the two hands. This is the type of hand that lends itself to a cross-ruff:

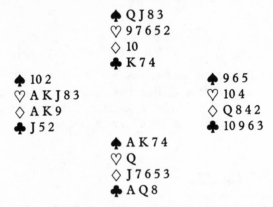

$$
\begin{array}{ccc}
 & \spadesuit\ Q J 8 3 & \\
 & \heartsuit\ 9 7 6 5 2 & \\
 & \diamondsuit\ 10 & \\
 & \clubsuit\ K 7 4 & \\
\spadesuit\ 10 2 & & \spadesuit\ 9 6 5 \\
\heartsuit\ A K J 8 3 & & \heartsuit\ 10 4 \\
\diamondsuit\ A K 9 & & \diamondsuit\ Q 8 4 2 \\
\clubsuit\ J 5 2 & & \clubsuit\ 10 9 6 3 \\
 & \spadesuit\ A K 7 4 & \\
 & \heartsuit\ Q & \\
 & \diamondsuit\ J 7 6 5 3 & \\
 & \clubsuit\ A Q 8 & \\
\end{array}
$$

South is playing four spades after West has opened one heart. The defense starts with two rounds of hearts and South ruffs. It is clear that if he draws three rounds of trumps declarer will fall short of ten tricks. He must plan to make his trumps separately.

The first move is to give up a diamond trick and the best return for the defense is a trump. South wins in his own hand and then cashes three rounds of clubs. Then he cross-ruffs the red suits. He makes, in all, seven tricks in spades and three in clubs.

Cashing the high cards in the fourth suit before setting about the cross-ruff is an important principle in the technique of cross-ruff play. Had declarer not cashed the clubs, East would have discarded that suit when declarer led hearts from the table, and South would have been unable thereafter to cash his club winners.

Another safety move in cross-ruff play is a high cross-ruff that avoids the danger of an overruff:

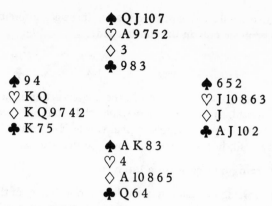

```
              ♠ Q J 10 7
              ♡ A 9 7 5 2
              ◊ 3
              ♣ 9 8 3
♠ 9 4                          ♠ 6 5 2
♡ K Q                          ♡ J 10 8 6 3
◊ K Q 9 7 4 2                  ◊ J
♣ K 7 5                        ♣ A J 10 2
              ♠ A K 8 3
              ♡ 4
              ◊ A 10 8 6 5
              ♣ Q 6 4
```

West opens the bidding with one diamond and South eventually plays at three spades. The king of hearts is led and dummy wins.

Clearly declarer must plan a cross-ruff but there is a danger that he may be overruffed by one defender or the other. The best play is to ruff a heart with the three of trumps at trick two, then cash ace of diamonds and cross-ruff with the high trumps. After making the three of trumps and five high ones in that way, declarer will have the single eight of trumps in his own hand and the single seven in dummy. One of these cards will make a trick on the cross-ruff and declarer will thus be sure of seven trump tricks and the two red aces.

CUE-BID IN OPPONENTS' SUIT

The strongest overcall in all approach-forcing systems is an immediate cue-bid of a suit that the opponents have already bid:

South	West	North	East
Pass	Pass	1♡	2♡

East's two hearts, sometimes called an immediate overcall, is unconditionally forcing to game in most systems. But others, including Culbertson, allow the bidding to be dropped short of game if the responder is hopelessly weak.

Some systems require specific holdings in the suit overcalled in addition to a very powerful hand. Thus, Goren requires an ace or void in that suit and uses the bid mainly as a slam try. Culbertson mentions an ace, void or singleton. The modern tendency, however, is not to require any specific holding in the suit overcalled.

When the opponents have called two suits there is a choice of suits in which to overcall, and most experts agree that a game-forcing overcall can now be made only in the suit last bid:

South	West	North	East
1♣	Pass	1♠	2♣

On this basis, East's two clubs in the above auction is not a game-forcing overcall. It promises a playable club suit but need be no stronger than the partnership's normal two-level overcall. The game-forcing overcall, in this sequence, would be two spades.

Game-forcing overcalls on a later round

A game-forcing overcall can be made at various stages of the auction. Here it is made by a player whose partner has made a natural call:

South	West	North	East
1♡	2♣	Pass	2♡

East's two hearts is game-forcing. It does not necessarily agree on clubs as the trump suit. More frequently, this type of game-forcing overcall is used when there seems to be a choice of game contracts and the player wishes to explore the alternatives.

The responder to a take-out double may also use the overcall of the opponent's suit:

South	West	North	East
1♠	Double	Pass	2♠

East's two spades is generally played as forcing to game.

For alternative uses of the overcall in an opponent's suit, see *Astro Cue-Bid, Colorful Cue-Bid,* and *Michaels Cue-Bid.*

CUE-BID TO SHOW CONTROLS

A cue-bid promises first-round control in the suit named and generally amounts to a slam suggestion.

Two conditions must apply before a cue-bid can be made:

(a) It must be clear from the previous bidding that the cue-bidder cannot wish to play in the suit named.

(b) The level at which the cue-bid is made must be such that the partnership is committed to game, at least.

Thus, in the following auction four clubs is a cue-bid:

	South	North
	1◇	1♠
	3♠	4♣

North cannot want to play in clubs, and since any call commits the partnership to game, four clubs must be a slam suggestion.

In the next auction three clubs is *not* a cue-bid, because the partnership is not committed to game:

	South	North
	1♡	2♡
	3♣	

Three clubs is merely a try for game (see *Trial Bid*).

When a player has more than one control he will generally cue-bid the one that can be shown at the lowest level (four clubs in preference to four hearts, three spades in preference to four clubs).

A bid in the opponents' suit does not necessarily promise first-round control. In many systems it is used merely as a game force (see *Cue-Bid in Opponents' Suit*).

Responding to cue-bids

A cue-bid is not a conventional bid and does not demand a conventional response. It gives information and invites partner to do the same. The responder to a cue-bid has to judge whether or not his values look good, in the light of the previous bidding.

(a) **If his values are relatively good** he may make a fresh cue-bid or take other strong action.

(b) **If his values are relatively poor** he can return to the agreed suit at the minimum level.

(c) **In borderline cases** he may make a fresh cue-bid provided this does not increase the level of the contract. Thus:

	South	North
	1♠	3♠
	4◇	?

If North has little in reserve for his three-spade call he will not show club control by cue-bidding five clubs. But he may call four hearts if he has heart control, for that does not carry the bidding beyond four spades.

Cue-bidding second-round controls

After first-round control of a suit has been shown by a cue-bid, a subsequent cue-bid in that suit by either player shows second-round control.

When no other convenient slam try is available a player may cue-bid in a suit of which he holds only second-round control. That is a matter of partnership understanding.

CULBERTSON FOUR-FIVE NO-TRUMP

Introduced as part of the Culbertson system in the early 1930's, this was the first convention to attach a special meaning to a bid of 4 NT. In the United States it has lost ground to the simpler Blackwood convention.

The Culbertson 4-5 differs from Blackwood in that it gives, as well as seeks, information. Also, there is more latitude for the exercise of judgment in selecting the response to 4 NT.

Qualifications for 4 NT

A conventional bid of 4 NT guarantees three aces, or two aces and a king of a suit bid by the partnership.

Only genuine suits rank in determining what is a suit previously bid by the partnership. Suits that have been bid artificially do not count (for example, a conventional two-club opening, or an overcall in an opponent's suit, or a cue-bid).

Responses to 4 NT

(a) Lacking an ace, or the kings of all bid suits, responder signs off by calling five in the lowest genuine suit that has been bid by either partner.

(b) With an ace or a void of an unbid suit, he bids five in that suit. But he has the option of signing off instead if his judgment tells him that a brake should be applied. That may happen when the control is in a suit of higher rank than the agreed trump suit.

(c) With an ace of a bid suit, or with the kings of all bid suits, he bids six in the agreed trump suit, or five of a suit which is not the lowest valued. But again he may use his judgment and sign off instead.

(d) With two aces, or one ace and the kings of all the bid suits, the response is 5 NT.

4 NT followed by 5 NT

A player who holds the four aces can show them by calling 4 NT and following with 5 NT after partner has signed off.

A direct call of 5 NT

A player who, bypassing 4 NT, bids a direct 5 NT, shows at least three aces and a king of a bid suit. The sign-off is now six of the agreed trump suit and there are no other conventional responses.

Many players do not use 5 NT in this sense but reserve it instead for the grand slam force.

CULBERTSON SYSTEM

The latest version of the Culbertson system, published soon after the author's death in 1955, differed little from the standard methods described in this book. The most important differences are set out below.

Responses to 1 NT opening

The opening 1 NT bid is strong, as in standard practice, but a simple response of two in a suit is forcing for one round—not a weak bid as in Goren and Acol. Also, Culbertson never adopted the artificial two-club response to 1 NT.

Forcing and non-forcing sequences

There are some sequences that are classified in Culbertson as invitational but are now treated as forcing in standard American practice. These are examples:

South	North
1♡	2◇
3♣	

South	North
1♠	2♣
3♠	

South	North
1♣	1♠
1 NT	3♠

South	North
1◇	1♡
1♠	3◇

In *Standard American* all these sequences are forcing. In Culbertson they are strong, but none of them is by definition forcing.

Jump overcalls

Culbertson never adopted the weak jump overcall that is now played in Goren and most other American systems. He played the jump overcall as strong but not forcing.

Special conventions

Culbertson introduced many special conventions which are often used independently of his system. See *Asking-Bids, Culbertson Four-Five No-Trump* and *Trump Asking-Bids*.

DECEPTIVE LEAD

A deceptive opening lead is one that departs from normal convention with the object of misleading the declarer. For example, if a player normally leads the king from a suit headed by the ace and king, to lead the ace instead would be a deceptive lead.

The lead of an unorthodox card from a sequence is a common form of deceptive lead, particularly in the trump suit. The jack, from Q J bare, in the hope that declarer will finesse for the queen on the second round, is too well known to have any element of surprise, but there are other positions of a similar kind:

Q 6 4

10 9   J 3 2

A K 8 7 5

If West leads the nine and declarer treats that as a true card he may go up with dummy's queen and play East for J 10 3 2. This is a variation of the same play:

J 6 4

10 9 3   K 2

A Q 8 7 5

On the lead of the nine declarer may put up the jack, placing East with K 10 x.

In the plain suits a deceptive card may be in order when leading from strength through strength in a situation such as the following:

A K 9 5

Q J 10 3   8 2

7 6 4

Against no trump West deems it necessary to attack here but suspects that dummy may be strong in the suit. If West leads the jack, declarer may play East for Q x and lay down ace and king.

When dummy is expected to hold the king, the queen from A Q x can be an effective play. Dummy may duck and the defenders gain a tempo.

Leads to misrepresent length

A well-tried stratagem against no trump is the lead of the fifth best card instead of the normal fourth best. That sometimes works well on hands of the following kind:

(See hand on next page.)

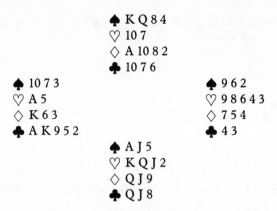

```
                  ♠ K Q 8 4
                  ♡ 10 7
                  ◇ A 10 8 2
                  ♣ 10 7 6
♠ 10 7 3                          ♠ 9 6 2
♡ A 5                             ♡ 9 8 6 4 3
◇ K 6 3                           ◇ 7 5 4
♣ A K 9 5 2                       ♣ 4 3
                  ♠ A J 5
                  ♡ K Q J 2
                  ◇ Q J 9
                  ♣ Q J 8
```

South opens 1 NT, West passes, and North raises to 3 NT. In view of his own strength, West judges that his partner will not be seriously concerned in the defense and that to mislead him will do no harm. West, therefore, leads the two of clubs instead of the five or a high one.

If declarer treats the two of clubs as a true card he will think it safe to play hearts and will be defeated.

Suppose, on the other hand, that West led the five of clubs. Dummy plays low and East plays the three. Now declarer will place West with at least a five-card suit (since the two is missing) and will take the diamond finesse rather than attack the hearts.

That gambit has a corollary that is perhaps less well known: a defender can sometimes play on declarer's nerves by leading his third best card from a four-card suit, giving declarer the impression that the lead is from a five-card suit.

In an expert game, where the declarer will note every card and will try to count the hand, a player may sometimes make unorthodox leads of that kind against a trump call, as well as against no trump.

DECEPTIVE PLAY

The field of deceptive play ranges wide, from a complete tactical plan to the right choice of card in a single suit. Here are some examples of deceptive play within a narrow range:

Plays to conceal strength

When the defenders open a suit in which the declarer is well up-holstered, they can sometimes be persuaded to continue along the same track.

Q 9 x x x   10 x

A K J

Defending against no trump, West leads low and East plays the ten.
If declarer has a more serious weakness in another suit he can win
with the king or ace, not the jack. That will give West the impression
that his partner holds J 10.

When declarer's own long suit is opened up, it can be good deception
to hold up for one round.

x x

10 8 x x   K x

A Q J 5 2

South has concealed this suit in the bidding and West leads low to his
partner's king. If South takes the trick and clears the suit, the defenders
will look for a weakness elsewhere. South does better to allow the king
to hold, dropping the five. East will surely continue and South will have
saved a tempo.

The same sort of play can be made by a defender:

Q 10 9 x

x   A K J x x

x x x

At no trump, declarer leads low and finesses the nine. East plays low
and waits for South to repeat the performance.

Plays to conceal weakness

An old stratagem at no-trump play, but one that still has its successes, is for declarer to simulate strength in a suit where he most fears an attack. For example, with 10 x x in dummy and J x in the closed hand, declarer enters dummy to lead up to the jack. Left-hand may win and open up another suit.

At trump contracts, deceptive play may be called for when a defender is after a ruff. When declarer recognizes that the opening lead is probably a singleton he must consider which card from his own hand will best conceal the situation from the other defender. For example:

K 8 5 2

3   A Q 7 6 4

J 10 9

South plays at a trump call and this is a suit that has not been mentioned in the bidding. West leads the three, dummy plays low and East puts on the queen.

Now, if South plays either the jack or the nine, East will reflect that his partner would not lead the three from J 10 3 or from 10 9 3. South, therefore, must drop the ten, the only card that may leave East in some doubt. After the play of the ten East may not be sure whether the three is a singleton or from J 9 3. Again:

J x x

A Q x x x x   2

K 10 x

This is a side suit in which West has overcalled at the range of two. West leads the ace and South, judging that East's two is a singleton, drops the king. That may look to West like a singleton and he may not continue the suit.

Leading towards the closed hand

In establishing a suit, declarer can sometimes improve his chances by leading from dummy instead of from his own hand:

                          A Q x x

        J 10 x x   K x

                          x x x

The first play should be a small card from the table, holding the queen finesse in reserve. In the diagram position East may put up the king.

There are many positions of that kind where a lead from the table may induce a defensive error.

Some examples of false-carding by the defenders are described under that title, and some deceptive ways of broaching a new suit are mentioned under *Deceptive Lead*. Another kind of deception is described under *Crashing Honors*.

DELAYED GAME RAISE

This is a technique that can be used in responding to an opening bid of one in a major suit. The responder makes a simple take-out on the first round, then follows with a jump to game in opener's first-bid suit. For example:

South	North
1♠	2♣
2♡	4♠

South	North
1♠	2♦
3♦	4♠

South	North
1♡	2♣
2 NT	4♡

In each of the above sequences, North's second bid is a delayed game raise. It promises strong trump support, at least four cards, and more honor strength than an immediate raise to four would have shown.

Thus, the delayed game raise can be used to describe the sort of hand that is rather too strong for a direct raise to game, but is not quite strong enough for a jump-shift. For example, South opens one spade and North holds:

♠ A Q x x   ♡ A J x   ◇ x x   ♣ K x x x

Playing the delayed game raise, North would respond two clubs and would bid four spades on the next round. That would be understood to show a hand of this general character.

Delayed game raises are a useful addition to bidding technique when raises to three are limit-bids and not forcing. See also *Swiss Convention*.

DESCHAPELLES COUP

This is a defensive play named after a champion of whist. It consists of the sacrifice of a high card to establish an entry to partner's hand:

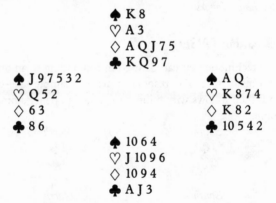

                    ♠ K 8
                    ♡ A 3
                    ◇ A Q J 7 5
                    ♣ K Q 9 7
    ♠ J 9 7 5 3 2   ♠ A Q
    ♡ Q 5 2   ♡ K 8 7 4
    ◇ 6 3   ◇ K 8 2
    ♣ 8 6   ♣ 10 5 4 2
                    ♠ 10 6 4
                    ♡ J 10 9 6
                    ◇ 10 9 4
                    ♣ A J 3

South is in 3 NT and West leads the five of spades. East wins the first two tricks with the ace and queen.

Recognizing that the only hope is to find an entry to partner's hand, East switches to the king of hearts—the Deschapelles Coup. It makes no difference whether declarer takes the ace at once or holds up for one round: East, when he comes in with the king of diamonds, will be able to put partner in with the queen of hearts.

For a similar play, see *Merrimac Coup*.

DEVIL'S COUP

The French phrase, *coup de diable*, is used for a play in which a defender's trump winner is made to vanish in magical fashion.

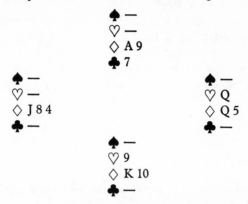

```
              ♠ —
              ♡ —
              ◇ A 9
              ♣ 7
♠ —                        ♠ —
♡ —                        ♡ Q
◇ J 8 4                    ◇ Q 5
♣ —                        ♣ —
              ♠ —
              ♡ 9
              ◇ K 10
              ♣ —
```

Diamonds are trump and the defenders, with J x x in one hand, Q x in the other, appear to have a natural trump trick. However, on the lead of the nine of hearts by South the best that West can do is ruff with the jack. Dummy overruffs and the ten of trump is finessed on the way back.

The ending arose from the following hand:

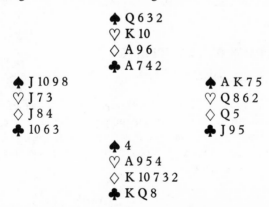

```
              ♠ Q 6 3 2
              ♡ K 10
              ◇ A 9 6
              ♣ A 7 4 2
♠ J 10 9 8                 ♠ A K 7 5
♡ J 7 3                    ♡ Q 8 6 2
◇ J 8 4                    ◇ Q 5
♣ 10 6 3                   ♣ J 9 5
              ♠ 4
              ♡ A 9 5 4
              ◇ K 10 7 3 2
              ♣ K Q 8
```

The contract is. six diamonds. South loses the first trick to the jack of spades and ruffs the continuation. He follows with three rounds of clubs, a spade ruff, and three rounds of hearts, ruffing on the table. Then the last spade is ruffed and he has the position shown above.

DOUBLE-BARRELED STAYMAN

An extension of the *Stayman Convention* whereby both two clubs and two diamonds in response to 1 NT are conventional, asking primarily for major suit length.

Two clubs is the weaker response. Any continuation by the two club bidder is non-forcing. A jump to three hearts or three spades on the second round is only invitational.

Two diamonds over 1 NT is forcing to game. The opener shows a four-card major, rebids 2 NT, or may jump to three with a five-card suit.

Compare *Gladiator Convention*.

DOUBLE FINESSE

A double finesse is one that will win the trick if two enemy cards are favorably placed:

A Q 10

x x x

A finesse of the ten is a double finesse against the king and jack.
See also *Combination Finesse*.

DOUBLE RAISE OF SUIT OPENING

Major suit opening

A double raise of a major suit opening is forcing to game in *Standard American*. It promises good trump support (at least four cards) and, roughly speaking, a hand as strong as a minimum opening bid.

The requirements are unchanged if an opponent overcalls the major suit opening. For example:

South	West	North	East
1♠	2◇	3♠	Pass

North's bid of three spades is forcing, according to Goren. Many players prefer to use limit-raises (see *Limit-Bids*) in a competitive situation, as it may otherwise be difficult to express a hand that is just too good for a single raise.

The double raise is not forcing when made by a player who has already passed.

See also *Two No-Trump or Three No-Trump as Artificial Raise.*

Double raise of a minor suit

Traditionally, a raise from one to three in a minor is also game-forcing. Here, again, the modern tendency is to treat it as a natural raise on a hand that presents no good alternative. See also *Inverted Minor Suit Raises.*

DOUBLE SQUEEZE

A squeeze that involves both opponents is called a double squeeze. This is the purest and shortest form:

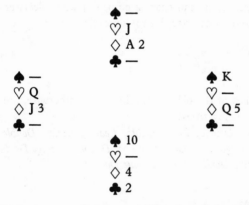

South leads the two of clubs and West has to throw a diamond in order to keep the queen of hearts in front of dummy's jack. Then the jack of hearts is discarded and East is squeezed in spades and diamonds.

For the double squeeze to operate in so economical a space, the two one-card threats, ♡J and ♠10 in this example, must both be favorably positioned, on the left of the opponent whom they threaten.

In the above example the squeeze was simultaneous, inasmuch as both opponents were squeezed on the same trick. When the squeeze operates on successive tricks it is called non-simultaneous. This is one of many variations:

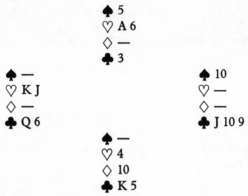

The threat cards are not so favorably placed for declarer as in the previous example, but there is compensation in the presence of an extra entry. On the lead of the ten of diamonds West has to throw a club, so the six of hearts is discarded from dummy. East is not yet under pressure, for he can spare a club, but when declarer continues with a heart to dummy's ace, East is squeezed in turn.

DOUBLES

Various types of double, conventional and otherwise, are discussed under the following titles:

Co-operative Double, Free Double, Lead-Directing Double, Lightner Slam Double, Negative Double, Optional Double, Penalty Double, Penalty Pass, Responsive Double and *Take-out Double*.

DRURY CONVENTION

Devised by Douglas Drury of San Francisco, formerly from Canada, this convention provides a safety cover for sub-minimum opening bids in certain situations. It is popular with duplicate players, who are more partial to light openings than are rubber bridge players.

The convention operates only over an opening one heart or one spade in third or fourth position. The responder, who has previously passed, bids an artificial two clubs. If the opener is in fact sub-minimum he rebids two diamonds. Any rebid other than two diamonds establishes a genuine opening. With a diamond suit and a fair hand the opener may also bid two diamonds for the moment, as this artificial bid will never be passed. On the next round he will clarify the situation.

Here are two examples that show the use of the convention. South deals and passes on:

(1)　♠ A Q 8 5　　♡ K 9 7 3　　◇ 10 8 2　　♣ J 2

North opens third hand with one heart or one spade. South is too strong for a single raise, but a double raise may lead to a minus score if partner is weak. South therefore bids two clubs and, over a rebid of two diamonds, bids simply two hearts.

(2)　♠ K 9　　♡ Q 10 9 3　　◇ K J 8 2　　♣ Q 10 8

North has opened fourth hand with one spade. The natural response of 2 NT may take the bidding too high or it may by-pass a better contract in hearts. Playing Drury, South responds two clubs and bids two hearts over two diamonds. If the opener has a weak hand with long spades he bids two spades now, and the bidding ends.

DUCKING

A player is said to duck when he concedes an early trick in a suit with a view to maintaining communication and running more tricks later on. The withholding of a winning card for other tactical reasons is more correctly termed a hold-up.

This is the simplest example of ducking:

A K 10 x x

x x

Lacking an outside entry to the North hand, declarer's only chance to bring home this suit is to duck the first round and play for a three-three break.

It might be right to duck even if there were plentiful entries outside the long suit. To play the ace, king and a small card would establish tricks for the opponents in the event of a bad break, whereas by ducking the first round declarer retains a measure of control. This may be especially important if the suit is trump.

There is an old maxim: "Duck as high as you can afford." In the example above, that would mean that the ten should be played, gaining a trick when West, holding queen and jack, had played low.

This is a more advanced situation of the same type:

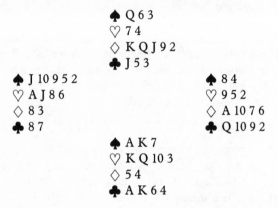

```
                    ♠ Q 6 3
                    ♡ 7 4
                    ◇ K Q J 9 2
                    ♣ J 5 3
  ♠ J 10 9 5 2                      ♠ 8 4
  ♡ A J 8 6                         ♡ 9 5 2
  ◇ 8 3                             ◇ A 10 7 6
  ♣ 8 7                             ♣ Q 10 9 2
                    ♠ A K 7
                    ♡ K Q 10 3
                    ◇ 5 4
                    ♣ A K 6 4
```

West leads the jack of spades against 3 NT and South wins. If South plays a diamond to dummy's king, East will hold up and declarer will be held to two tricks in the suit because of lack of communication.

Needing only three tricks from diamonds, South should duck a round at trick two. When he regains the lead he knocks out the diamond ace, and the queen of spades provides an entry to the table.

Ducking play can be equally effective in defense. The following is a standard situation:

```
            K Q 8


7 4                                 A 6 5 3 2


            J 10 9
```

South is playing a trump contract and this is a side suit. West, who has a trump entry, leads his doubleton and East, who has no other entry, ducks to maintain communication. Later, West may come in and obtain a third-round ruff.

The maneuver shown in the next example is more common at no trump:

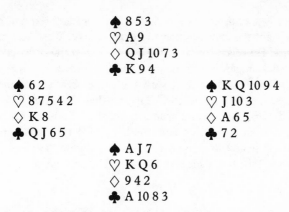

♠ 8 5 3
♡ A 9
◇ Q J 10 7 3
♣ K 9 4

♠ 6 2
♡ 8 7 5 4 2
◇ K 8
♣ Q J 6 5

♠ K Q 10 9 4
♡ J 10 3
◇ A 6 5
♣ 7 2

♠ A J 7
♡ K Q 6
◇ 9 4 2
♣ A 10 8 3

South plays in 3 NT after East has overcalled in spades. West leads the six of spades and we will suppose, first, that East puts up the queen. South will hold off, and as East has only one entry the suit will be dead.

The correct play is for East to play the nine of spades on the opening lead. South wins with the jack and leads a diamond. The difference now is that West can go up with the king of diamonds and lead his second spade while East still has an entry.

DUMMY REVERSAL

Declarer is said to reverse the dummy when he uses his own trumps for ruffing and later uses dummy's trumps to draw those of the opponents. To put it another way, he makes dummy the master hand.

Whereas, in general, there is advantage only in ruffing in the shorter hand, in a true dummy reversal an extra trick is developed by ruffing several times in the long hand:

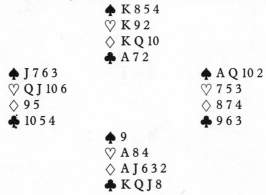

♠ K 8 5 4
♡ K 9 2
◇ K Q 10
♣ A 7 2

♠ J 7 6 3
♡ Q J 10 6
◇ 9 5
♣ 10 5 4

♠ A Q 10 2
♡ 7 5 3
◇ 8 7 4
♣ 9 6 3

♠ 9
♡ A 8 4
◇ A J 6 3 2
♣ K Q J 8

South is playing six diamonds and West leads the queen of hearts. At first sight the contract seems to depend upon West holding the ace of spades. However, by executing a dummy reversal declarer can make twelve tricks regardless of the position of that card.

South wins the first trick with the ace of hearts and immediately leads a spade towards dummy. Suppose that East wins and returns a heart: dummy wins and a spade is ruffed by South. Then follows a diamond to dummy's ten and another spade ruff, this time with a high trump in case West is short of spades; dummy is re-entered with a trump and the last spade is ruffed high. The position now is:

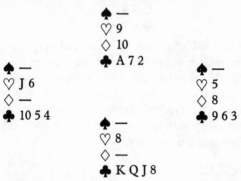

Declarer plays a club to the ace and draws East's trump, throwing his own losing heart. What has happened, in effect, is that by dummy reversal the declarer has extended the length of his trump suit from five to six: three ruffs in hand and three top trumps on the table.

When the defenders adopt forcing tactics, dummy reversal may sometimes be employed as a counter-stroke.

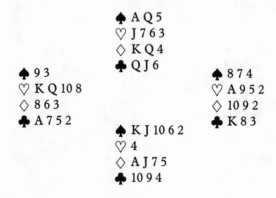

At four spades South is in no difficulty unless the defenders play a forcing game. On any lead but a heart he has time to draw trumps and establish a club for his tenth trick.

Suppose, however, that West starts with two rounds of hearts. South accepts the force and goes on to ruff dummy's remaining hearts, using spades and diamonds as entries to dummy. After ruffing three times, he enters dummy to draw the outstanding trump, discarding a club from hand. Thus he never makes a club trick, but makes an extra trump by way of dummy reversal.

ECHO (OR PETER)

This is the name for the "high-low" method of signaling in defense, to show strength or certain features of distribution.

To show strength

The play of a higher card followed by a lower one in the same suit shows strength and is often a request to partner to lead the suit, or to continue it. It is also known as a "come-on" signal. This message holds good however low the cards. It is possible to echo by playing a three followed by a two.

Sometimes a defender can make only one discard, and in that case a single high card may be a sign of strength. In general, to discard or to follow suit with a seven or higher card is an encouragement to partner. When a defender has a suit such as A K 5 3 2 the best he can do, if there is opportunity for only one discard, is to play the 5; an observant partner will note that smaller cards are missing.

To show a doubleton in a trump contract

At a trump contract the echo in a plain suit is used to show a doubleton as well as to show strength. The echo tells partner that the player can ruff the third round.

On the lead of a king from a suit headed by ace-king, a partner who desires a continuation will echo with J x but not with Q x. There is a widely accepted convention that the play of the queen under the king shows that the Q J is held and that it is safe for the partner to underlead on the next round.

To show distribution at no trump

The echo is also used to signal length at no trump. It shows an even number of cards, usually two or four, in the suit that is being played. This signal is especially useful when declarer is attempting to establish a long suit in dummy:

K J 10 7 4

A 8 5   9 3

Q 6 2

Having no obvious side entry to the table, South leads the queen, West plays low, and East plays the nine. Reading the nine as the beginning of an echo, West knows that he must hold up again on the second round.

Now take a slightly different position:

K J 10 7 4

A 8 5   9 3 2

Q 6

This time East plays the two on the first round. That marks him with three cards and West can afford to take the ace on the second round.

In the next example a defender echoes with four cards:

K Q 10 9 6 3

8 7 5 2   A 4

J

Declarer leads the jack, West plays the seven, and North the queen. From the play of the seven East can read his partner for two cards or four: if it were two, declarer would have three and there would be no advantage in holding up, so East assumes that West has four and takes the ace immediately.

See also *Trump Echo*.

ELIMINATION

The term elimination play is used especially for that form of end-play in which a defender is forced either to lead into a tenace or to concede a ruff and discard. Before the throw-in takes place, declarer has to eliminate from his own hand and from dummy the suits that a defender could safely play.

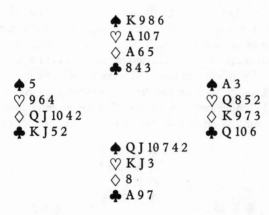

```
                    ♠ K 9 8 6
                    ♡ A 10 7
                    ◇ A 6 5
                    ♣ 8 4 3
  ♠ 5                                   ♠ A 3
  ♡ 9 6 4                               ♡ Q 8 5 2
  ◇ Q J 10 4 2                          ◇ K 9 7 3
  ♣ K J 5 2                             ♣ Q 10 6
                    ♠ Q J 10 7 4 2
                    ♡ K J 3
                    ◇ 8
                    ♣ A 9 7
```

Against four spades West leads out the queen of diamonds. South wins in dummy, ruffs a diamond, and leads a trump. East wins and plays a club; South takes the ace, enters dummy with a trump, and ruffs dummy's last diamond.

Having drawn trumps and eliminated diamonds, South throws the lead with a club. The defenders can cash two club tricks but then have to lead a heart or concede a ruff and discard.

An elimination of that kind, which is sure to succeed against any lie of the cards, is called a perfect elimination. Sometimes declarer is unable to achieve that ideal and has to rely on a partial or imperfect elimination which depends for its success on a reasonably favorable distribution. Here is an example of a partial elimination:

(See hand on next page.)

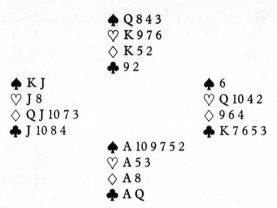

♠ Q 8 4 3
♥ K 9 7 6
♦ K 5 2
♣ 9 2

♠ K J
♥ J 8
♦ Q J 10 7 3
♣ J 10 8 4

♠ 6
♥ Q 10 4 2
♦ 9 6 4
♣ K 7 6 5 3

♠ A 10 9 7 5 2
♥ A 5 3
♦ A 8
♣ A Q

South is in six spades and a diamond is led. Declarer wins and lays down the ace of trumps, and when the king does not fall he has to find a lucky lie of the other cards. A diamond is played to dummy's king and a diamond is ruffed. Then dummy is re-entered with the king of hearts and the club finesse taken. Now the ace of clubs and ace of hearts are cashed and declarer throws the lead with a trump. As the cards lie, the partial elimination succeeds, for West has no more hearts and has to give a ruff and discard. A more advanced example of partial elimination:

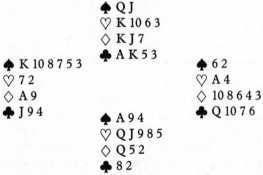

♠ Q J
♥ K 10 6 3
♦ K J 7
♣ A K 5 3

♠ K 10 8 7 5 3
♥ 7 2
♦ A 9
♣ J 9 4

♠ 6 2
♥ A 4
♦ 10 8 6 4 3
♣ Q 10 7 6

♠ A 9 4
♥ Q J 9 8 5
♦ Q 5 2
♣ 8 2

Against four hearts West plays ace and another diamond. Realizing the danger of a diamond ruff, declarer seeks to improve his prospects by partial elimination.

Three rounds of clubs are played off, South ruffing the third round. East wins the next trick with the ace of hearts and gives his partner the ruff in diamonds. Now the advantage of the partial elimination is seen: West has only spades left and must lead away from the king.

ENTRY-KILLING PLAY

There are a number of plays by second hand which have the effect of killing or disrupting the declarer's entries to a long suit in the opposite hand. These plays are important when there are no other entries.

A J 10 5

K 7 3   Q 8 4

9 6 2

South leads the two, intending to play the ten from dummy. By going up with the king, West holds declarer to two tricks.

A J 9 6 3

Q 10 5   K 8 4

7 2

On the lead of the two West must go up with the queen. Otherwise, declarer will put on the nine and East will either have to let this win or give South a chance to make four tricks by finessing the jack on the next round.

The same kind of play is available to declarer at the expense of the defenders:

Q 10 5

7 2   A J 9 6 3

K 8 4

Suppose that West leads the seven against a no-trump contract. If he can read the position, declarer can break the run of the suit by going in with dummy's queen.

For other plays concerned with entry, see *Avoidance Play*, *Blocking*

Play, *Deschapelles Coup*, *Ducking*, *Hold-up Play*, *Merrimac Coup*, *Scissors Coup* and *Unblocking Play*.

ENTRY SQUEEZE

When a suit is blocked so that declarer cannot conveniently go from hand to hand, he can sometimes exert pressure on the opponents to compel them to provide the entry. That is an entry squeeze.

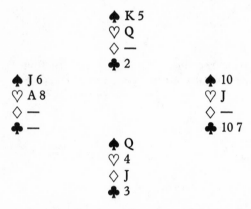

Playing at no trump, South requires three of the last four tricks. In a sense he has them, but the spades are blocked. On the lead of the jack of diamonds, however, West has to let go a heart, for otherwise the queen of spades can be overtaken. When West discards the eight of hearts, South cashes the queen of spades and exits with a heart, forcing West to give dummy the last trick.

This type of squeeze has numerous subdivisions. Compare the *Jettison Squeeze*.

FALSE-CARDING

For the defenders there are many well-established conventions in play. When, for example, a defender leads from Q J 10 the conventional play is the queen. When his partner leads the suit and next hand plays low, convention directs that the ten be played.

When a defender departs from convention with a view to misleading the declarer he is said to false-card. This is a simple example:

56

A J 10 x

x x x   K Q

x x x x

South leads low and finesses the jack. The conventional card for East is the queen, the lower of cards in sequence. If East false-cards, winning with the king, he may encourage declarer to think that a second finesse will succeed.

In these situations good players vary their game, playing sometimes a true card, sometimes a false card. The disadvantage of being a perpetual false-carder can be observed in an example such as the following:

A J 8 5 4

10 9 6   Q 2

K 7 3

For declarer, the normal play is to lay down the king and follow with a finesse of the jack. But on the lead of the king East drops the two and East is known to be an inveterate false-carder who, from 10 2 or 9 2, would surely drop the higher card. Now South can judge that the two can only be a singleton or from Q 2. Therefore, on the next round he goes up with the ace.

Obligatory false cards

On the other hand, there is a group of plays in which the defender must false-card in order to give declarer a guess:

J 9 x

x x x   K 10

A Q x x x

Declarer leads low from the North hand. If East plays the ten, South will finesse the queen and will lay down the ace on the next round, felling the king and making all five tricks.

East must play the king on the first round; that creates the possibility that South will finesse dummy's nine on the way back. Here is a similar position:

Q 6 2

10 9 3   K 4

A J 8 7 5

Again declarer leads low from dummy. East plays low and South finesses the jack. In order to leave South with a choice of plays on the next round, West must drop the nine or ten. Then it will be open to South to cross to dummy and lead the queen, with a view to dropping the 10 9.

A more advanced variation of that theme is the following:

K 10 6 2

J 9 5 4   3

A Q 8 7

South lays down the ace. If West follows with a small card South will assuredly play the queen on the next round, discovering the finesse against the jack. West, therefore, must false-card with the nine on the first lead. Then South has a choice of playing either opponent for J x x x.

Declarer's false cards

A deceptive play by declarer is sometimes referred to as a false card, but the term is not appropriate. There is no such thing as a true card for declarer in the same way as there is for a defender, who normally follows convention. Some tricky maneuvers by the declarer are described under *Deceptive Play*.

FINESSE

A finesse is an attempt to profit from a favorable lie of the cards. A player tries to win or establish a trick with a card that is not the highest held by his side. This is a simple finesse:

A Q

x x

South leads low and plays the queen from dummy, in the hope that the king lies with West.

K x x

J 10 9

Here South leads the jack and runs it if West does not cover.

By an extension of meaning, the term is also applied to situations such as this:

A x x

Q x x

North leads a small card to South's queen, this time playing East for the king.

A finesse that has already succeeded (for example, when the ten from K J 10 has fetched the ace) is called a marked finesse; if the opponent who is last to play has shown void, it is called a proven finesse. So far as the law (relating to a claim for tricks) is concerned, a proven finesse is still a finesse.

At trump contracts there is also the ruffing finesse:

K Q J x

Void

This is a plain suit and dummy leads the king. If East plays the ace South ruffs, but if East plays low the king is allowed to run—a ruffing finesse against East.

A finesse whose object is to gain an entry rather than win a trick is called an entry finesse.

A J x x

Q x x   10 x x x

K x

Suppose declarer does not need extra tricks from this suit, but requires two entries to dummy. He leads the small card and finesses the jack; on the second round, he overtakes the king with the ace.

As is often the case with an entry finesse, the defender, West, can thwart declarer's intention by going up with his high card on the first round of the suit.

See also *Backward Finesse, Combination Finesse, Double Finesse, Finesse against Dummy, Finesse against Partner* and *Two-way Finesse.*

FINESSE AGAINST DUMMY

When a defender, sitting over dummy, does not play third hand high but retains a card to head an honor on the table, he is said to finesse against dummy. This is a simple example:

K x x

x x x x   A J 10

Q x x

West leads a small card and dummy plays low; East inserts the ten, keeping a major tenace over dummy's king. East's finesse against dummy would also gain if West had underled the queen.

Another common example:

A 10 x

K 9 x x   J 8 x

Q x x

West leads small and dummy plays low. If East puts up the jack, South wins and can finesse dummy's ten, thus making three tricks in the suit.

If he were defending a suit contract East would not expect his partner to underlead the king-queen, so he would insert the eight instead of the jack. At no trump West might, in theory, have both king and queen; but that would leave declarer with nothing better than the nine, and on grounds of general probability the eight would still be the correct card for East to play.

The next example shows a still deeper finesse:

Q 9 5

J 8 6 4   A 10 7 3

K 2

Defending against no trump, West leads the four and dummy puts on the five. The Rule of Eleven tells East that South has only one card higher than the four. If it be the king, only the finesse of the seven will ensure holding declarer to one trick. Only if South had 8 2 would the seven be a mistake, and with that holding he would probably go up with the queen in dummy.

FINESSE AGAINST PARTNER

There are some occasions when a defender does not follow the rule, "Third hand high." A frequent example is when he finesses against dummy, as with A J 10 over dummy's K x x. See *Finesse against Dummy*.

61

When the defender declines to play high although dummy has no high card, he is said to finesse against his partner.

5 2

Q 10 9 8   K 7 4 3

A J 6

If West led the ten and East, placing declarer with A Q J, decided not to put up the king, that would be a costly mistake of the kind that has given rise to the maxim, "Never finesse against partner."

However, it can sometimes be good play to finesse against partner. One motive for so doing is to maintain communication, as in the following hand:

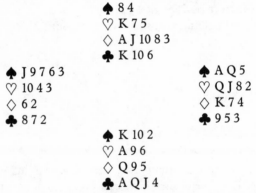

♠ 8 4
♡ K 7 5
♢ A J 10 8 3
♣ K 10 6

♠ J 9 7 6 3   ♠ A Q 5
♡ 10 4 3   ♡ Q J 8 2
♢ 6 2   ♢ K 7 4
♣ 8 7 2   ♣ 9 5 3

♠ K 10 2
♡ A 9 6
♢ Q 9 5
♣ A Q J 4

South opens 1 NT, North raises to 3 NT, and all pass. West leads the six of spades and it is not difficult for East to judge that his partner is unlikely to hold an entry for the long spades.

If East puts on the ace of spades and continues the suit, South will hold up the king until the third round and West's hand will be dead. East should, therefore, play the queen of spades at trick one. Not knowing who has the ace, South can hardly refuse to win; if he takes the trick, 3 NT will be defeated.

A finesse for discovery

There is another type of situation where it may pay to finesse against partner: when it is vital to place a particular card. For example:

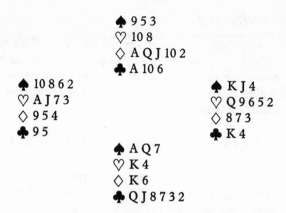

```
                  ♠ 9 5 3
                  ♡ 10 8
                  ◇ A Q J 10 2
                  ♣ A 10 6
  ♠ 10 8 6 2                      ♠ K J 4
  ♡ A J 7 3                       ♡ Q 9 6 5 2
  ◇ 9 5 4                         ◇ 8 7 3
  ♣ 9 5                           ♣ K 4
                  ♠ A Q 7
                  ♡ K 4
                  ◇ K 6
                  ♣ Q J 8 7 3 2
```

South is playing five clubs and West leads the two of spades. East can see that it is essential to take two tricks quickly in addition to the king of trump, but he cannot tell whether to try for two tricks in spades or in hearts.

By putting up the jack of spades at trick one, East escapes this dilemma. This is a finesse against partner that can hardly cost, for West would not underlead an ace against five clubs. When South wins with the queen of spades, East knows that when he comes in with the trump king he must switch to a heart.

FISHBEIN CONVENTION

This is a method devised by Harry Fishbein as a defense against a pre-emptive opening by an opponent.

Suppose that the opponent opens three hearts. An overcall of three spades, the next higher-ranking suit, is used in the Fishbein Convention as a request for partner to show his best suit. In the same way, three diamonds is used for a take-out over three clubs, three hearts over three diamonds and four clubs over three spades.

It follows that all other bids over an opponent's three-bid are natural. Double is for penalties and 3 NT is to play.

The convention can also be used against opponents' weak two-bids.

For alternative methods, see *Lower Minor Convention, Optional Double, Reese Defense,* and *Three No-Trump Take-out.*

FLINT CONVENTION

The object of this convention, devised by Jeremy Flint of London, is to enable the responder to a 2 NT opening to halt the bidding in three hearts or three spades. The first step is to respond three diamonds, directing the opener to bid three hearts. The convention would be used on a hand like this:

♠ 9 7 6 5 4 2   ♡ 4 3   ♢ 10 7   ♣ J 6 4

Over the forced rebid of three hearts, responder will transfer to three spades, which the opener is expected to pass. If the hearts and spades were reversed, responder would pass three hearts.

In "Extended Flint," an opener who is exceptionally strong in hearts, and prepared to play for game with any heart suit opposite, departs from the convention and bids three spades over three diamonds. Now if responder has hearts he goes to four hearts, but if his suit is spades he passes. When the 2 NT opener is prepared to play for game in *either* major he can bid 3 NT over three diamonds.

When the responder to 2 NT actually has diamonds he begins by responding three diamonds and then continues over the conventional rebid:

South	North
2 NT	3♢
3♡	3 NT

The sequence means that East has diamonds and is prepared to go beyond 3 NT.

FORCING BID

A forcing bid is one that requires the partner to keep the bidding open. The bid may be forcing to game or forcing for one round.

Game-forcing bids by opener

Most systems have a conventional opening bid that is forcing to game. In Goren any suit opening of two is game-forcing. In most other American systems an artificial two-club opening is forcing to game (except, in most cases, when the opener rebids 2 NT). In systems that use a strong one-club opening, like the *Schenken System*, the big bid is usually two diamonds.

On the second round of bidding a change of suit combined with a jump (see *Jump-Shift*) is game-forcing. So, in effect, is a jump rebid in a major suit after a response at the range of two:

South	North
1♠	2♣
3♠	

Game-forcing bids by responder

Any jump-shift:

South	North
1♡	3♣

A response of 2 NT:

South	North
1♡	2 NT

A double raise:

South	North		South	North
1♡	3♡	or	1♢	3♢

(But see *Double Raise of Suit Opening*.)

A jump preference at the three level:

South	North
1♢	1♡
1♠	3♢

Any continuation after a strong rebid:

South	North		South	North
1♦	1♡	or	1♦	1♡
2 NT	3♡ or 3♦		3♦	3♡

One-round forces by opener

A reverse after a response at the two level:

South	North
1♦	2♣
2♠	

A new suit at the range of three:

South	North
1♠	2♦
3♣	

One-round forces by responder

A simple take-out in a new suit (one spade over one heart, or two diamonds over one spade).

In most cases, a change of suit on the second round. That does not apply, however, when opener has rebid 1 NT and the new suit is not a reverse:

South	North
1♦	1♠
1 NT	2♡

Here two hearts is not forcing, as the opener's hand is strictly limited. See also *Fourth Suit Forcing* and *Trial Bid*.

FORCING PASS

A player is said to make a forcing pass when it is clear from the previous bidding that his partner will have to take some action. For example:

South	West	North	East
2 NT	Pass	3♠	4◇
Pass			

South has promised a very powerful hand and North has shown some values. It is not conceivable, therefore, that South should wish to defend a contract of four diamonds undoubled. South's pass is a forcing pass, saying, in effect, "My hand is reasonably well suited both to defending four diamonds doubled and to playing four spades. You choose!"

FORCING TACTICS (IN PLAY)

The defenders are said to play a forcing game when they set out to weaken declarer's trump holding by forcing him to ruff a side suit. Such tactics are often adopted when a defender has length in trumps and hopes to gain trump control.

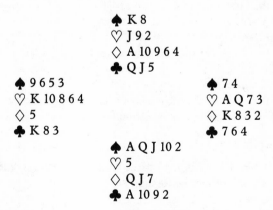

```
                     ♠ K 8
                     ♡ J 9 2
                     ◇ A 10 9 6 4
                     ♣ Q J 5
      ♠ 9 6 5 3                      ♠ 7 4
      ♡ K 10 8 6 4                   ♡ A Q 7 3
      ◇ 5                            ◇ K 8 3 2
      ♣ K 8 3                        ♣ 7 6 4
                     ♠ A Q J 10 2
                     ♡ 5
                     ◇ Q J 7
                     ♣ A 10 9 2
```

A forcing lead, a heart, is the only one to break four spades. After ruffing a heart and drawing trumps, declarer loses control when he takes a losing finesse in a minor suit.

On a club or spade lead, the hand is straightforward. On a diamond, declarer must play with care. He must go up with the ace and unblock with the queen or jack from hand. Then he draws trumps and leads his remaining diamond honor. If East wins, declarer takes four tricks in diamonds and six in the black suits; if East ducks, declarer switches to clubs.

As well as forcing declarer, defenders will sometimes force dummy. This may be necessary to protect a defender's trump holding against trump leads from dummy, or to shorten dummy's trumps so that declarer cannot draw trumps and still have an entry to dummy in the trump suit.

FORCING TWO-BIDS

An opening bid of two in a suit is forcing to game. The bid is also called the "demand two."

Goren two

In terms of the Goren point-count, the following are the requirements for an opening two-bid:
  25 points with a good five-card suit
  23 points with a good six-card suit
  21 points with a good seven-card suit

When the final contract is likely to be a minor suit, 2 points more are needed. Where there is a good secondary five-card suit, the requirements can be shaded by one point.

Goren two-bids are unconditionally forcing to game. The negative response is 2 NT. For a positive response partner needs 7 points with a quick trick, or 8 points with $\frac{1}{2}$ quick trick. Partner may also make a weak double raise of opener's suit to show good trump support but no card higher than a queen and no singleton.

Limit-two bid

In his later works Culbertson recommended that a single rebid of opener's suit should not be forcing:

South	North
2♠	2 NT
3♠	

Playing the limit-two, North can pass on complete weakness. This method removes some of the strain from opening bids of one, which otherwise have to cover a very wide range.

For an alternative method with strong hands, see *Two-Club Opening*.

FOUR-CLUB BLACKWOOD

Some players use four clubs instead of 4 NT as an inquiry for aces. Responses are on the "step" method—four diamonds shows no ace, and the bids from four hearts up to five clubs show from one to four aces respectively.

The convention cannot be used when there is any possibility that four clubs may be construed as a natural call. On all other occasions it has an advantage in gaining space. After the response to four clubs, five clubs can be used as an inquiry for kings, and even six clubs for queens. (Some partners arrange that where the response to four clubs is itself five clubs, showing four aces, some other conventional bid, such as 5 NT, should be used to ask for kings. A better arrangement is to respond four diamonds, not five clubs, when holding all four aces. Then five clubs is always available to ask for kings.)

Using four-club Blackwood, it is possible to identify a missing ace below the six-level. When partner has shown one or two aces by responding four hearts or four spades, the opener can use 4 NT as a means of inquiring, "Which ace or aces?" One ace can be shown by bidding the suit in which it is held. When responder has two aces he can identify them by a single call. The British writer, Norman Squire, suggests this method:

(a) If responder's aces are the same color, he bids five clubs.

(b) If of the same rank (both major or both minor), he bids five diamonds.

(c) If an "odd" combination, he bids five hearts.

It will be found that the 4 NT bidder, provided he has one ace himself, will always be able to determine which are the two aces opposite.

See also *Gerber Convention*.

FOURTH SUIT FORCING

The technique known as "fourth suit forcing," developed by players of the *Baron System*, has been adopted by most leading experts. The following account is derived from *Blueprint on Bidding* by Reese and Dormer.

"Fourth suit forcing," as a convention, means this: A bid of the fourth suit in an unopposed auction does not guarantee either length or strength in the suit named: it is merely a means of keeping the bidding alive.

South	North
1♠	2♣
2◇	2♡

North may have a suit of hearts, or he may have a singleton or doubleton.

The main object of the call is to keep several possibilities open where any other bid would be inaccurate and unsatisfactory. At the same time, it is constructive and forward-going. These are some examples:

(1) South	North
1♡	1♠
2♣	2◇

North holds:

♠ A K 8 7 5   ♡ 10 7   ◇ 9 5 3   ♣ A Q 2

Game is likely, but no good call is available over two clubs. A jump to four clubs would prejudice the chance of arriving at one of three other possible contracts.

(2) South	North
1♣	1◇
1♡	1♠

North holds:

♠ 10 4 3   ♡ K 6 2   ◇ A Q 8 4 3   ♣ A 6

Game is probable, but a natural three hearts would be by no means a happy reflection. Let West declare himself further over one spade.

(3) South	North
1♡	2♣
2◇	2♠

North holds:

♠ 9 2   ♡ J 3   ◇ 7 6   ♣ A K Q 7 5 4 2

Three clubs would be inadequate, four beyond the range of 3 NT. The bid of the fourth suit asks partner to bid no-trump if he has a guard in spades.

Responding to the fourth suit

The responder's duty is to make a descriptive bid, taking into account that his partner has his sights set on game. He will generally act as follows:

1. With a guard in the fourth suit, he will bid no-trump at an appropriate level.

2. With four cards in the fourth suit, he will generally raise from two to three. If the fourth suit has been bid at the three level, responder may prefer 3 NT.

3. If he has undisclosed values in one of his partner's suits, he will give delayed support.

4. Lacking any of these features, he will rebid a suit of his own.

FRAGMENT BID

A double jump in a new suit on the second round (one heart—one spade—four clubs) is used to indicate strong support for partner's last suit and a singleton or void in the unbid suit. There may be losers in the suit of the "fragment" bid. Compare *Out-of-the-Blue Cue-Bid*, where a similar effect is achieved by jumping in the suit where the control is held.

FREE BID

A player who responds to his partner's opening bid in face of an opponent's overcall is said to make a free bid. If his bid is a raise of his partner's suit, that is a free raise (see *Free Raise*).

Thus, in the following auction, North's one spade is a free bid:

South	West	North	East
1♣	1♡	1♠	Pass

The requirements for a free bid are higher than those for a simple response when there has been no overcall.

Free bids at the one-level

A free bid in a suit at the one-level promises at least 9 or 10 points, counting distributional points. The following would be a minimum hand for a free bid by North in the above auction:

♠ K Q x x x   ♡ x x x   ◇ K x x   ♣ x x

On the Goren count, the hand is worth 9 points, counting 1 point for distribution. If West had not overcalled, North could respond one spade without the king of diamonds.

Free bids at the two-level

When responder's suit is of a higher rank than the opener's, the standards for a free bid are higher than for a normal two-over-one response. Responder needs a count of 12 or 13 points, including distribution, for the bid of two spades in this sequence:

South	West	North	East
1♡	2♣	2♠	

Free bids over opponent's take-out double

When the opening bid is immediately followed by a take-out double, a free bid by the next player does not show extra values.

South	West	North	East
1◇	Double	1♠	Pass

North can be quite weak and the opening bidder is not forced to bid again.

See also *Free Rebid*.

FREE RAISE

When a player raises his partner's opening bid after an intervening call he is said to give a free raise. For example:

South	West	North	East
1♠	2◇	2♠	Pass

North's raise to two spades, made over the intervening call, is a free raise.

Free raise to the two-level

A free raise to the two-level, as in the above auction, promises sound values. The responder should pass the sort of hand on which he might otherwise have strained to keep the bidding open, for after the opponent's call the opening bidder will have a second chance to speak.

Some authorities, however, consider that it is tactically better to give a free raise on minimum hands with distributional strength, rather than to be left out of the auction altogether.

Raise over an opponent's take-out double

When the intervening call is a take-out double the situation is reversed. A raise is, if anything, weaker than if the opponent had passed.

South	West	North	East
1♠	Double	2♠	

North's two spades can be bid on a minimum, in an attempt to keep the opponents out. In the same way, a jump to three spades is limited. Stronger hands are dealt with by way of a redouble or a jump to game.

See also *Two No-Trump over a Double*.

FREE REBID

When the opening bidder calls freely on the second round, after an opponent's overcall, he is said to make a free rebid:

South	West	North	East
1♡	Pass	1♠	2♢
2♡			

East's overcall has relieved South of the obligation to keep the bidding alive and South's two heart call is therefore a free rebid. Since this is a voluntary action it is generally accepted that the free rebid should show better than minimum values.

GAMBLING THREE NO-TRUMP

See *Three No-Trump Opening*.

GAME TRY

See *Short-suit Game Tries* and *Trial Bids*.

GARDENER NO-TRUMP OVERCALL

The British international player, Nico Gardener, and his partners use an overcall of 1 NT as a two-way bid. It may be genuine, but more often it is made on a weak hand with an escape suit. If partner has the sort of hand on which he would take constructive action opposite a strong no-trump overcall, he bids two clubs. Then the overcaller bids 2 NT if genuine, two of his suit if not.

The object of the overcall is not so much to deceive, for its character is known to the opposition, as to interfere with the normal processes of constructive bidding. Being a form of *Controlled Psychic*, it enables a player with a long suit to enter the bidding without misleading his partner as to the general worth of his hand.

GERBER CONVENTION

In its original form, this was a device by John S. Gerber, of Houston, Texas, to discover the number of aces held by a player who had opened with a bid of 1 NT or 2 NT. It uses a bid of four clubs for this purpose, and the name is also applied to other variations of *Four Club Blackwood*.

Four clubs, as an immediate response to an opening bid of 1 NT or 2 NT, asks the opening bidder to show his aces in accordance with the step system. Four diamonds shows no ace, four hearts shows one ace, and so on.

If the four-club bidder next calls five clubs, that asks for kings to be shown in the same fashion. If he makes any call other than five clubs, that is a sign-off. For example:

South	North
1 NT	4♣ (Gerber)
4♠	4 NT

South's four-spade call shows two aces. North's 4 NT is *not* a demand bid. It is a sign-off in no trump.

The convention can also be used when 2 NT follows an artificial two-club opening:

South	North
2♣	2♡
2 NT	4♣

Here four clubs is Gerber, asking for aces.

See also *Four-Club Blackwood*.

GLADIATOR CONVENTION

Developed in New Zealand, this convention is designed for responding to a strong no trump. It covers a somewhat similar field as the Stayman Convention but in a more elaborate way.

In response to the 1 NT opening, a raise to 2 NT or 3 NT is natural. The following responses, however, are conventional:

Two clubs shows not more than one honor-trick. The opener must call two diamonds and the responder now signs off in his best suit.

Two diamonds is game-forcing and asks for major suits.

Two hearts or two spades is game-forcing and promises a minimum of $1\frac{1}{2}$ honor-tricks and a five-card suit.

Three-level responses show slam aspirations, with a minimum suit of Q x x x x.

Four-level responses also show slam hopes, but with a six-card or longer suit headed by the jack at best.

An overcall of 1 NT is made on the same strength as an opening 1 NT and the same system of conventional responses can be used.

Compare *Double-Barreled Stayman.*

GOREN POINT-COUNT

From a method devised by William Anderson, of Toronto, Goren has evolved a point-count method to cover suit as well as no-trump bidding.

For no-trump bidding, only high-card points are counted:

4 for each ace
3 for each king
2 for each queen
1 for each jack

For suit bidding the following distributional points are added:

3 for a void
2 for each singleton
1 for each doubleton

Adjustments when opening the bidding

A singleton honor is reduced in value by 1 point unless partner bids the suit.

Q J x is counted as only 2 points.

1 point is deducted for an aceless hand.

1 point is added when all four aces are held.

Revaluing

When a player has good support for his partner and proposes to raise, he adds the following "dummy points":

1 for a doubleton.

3 for a singleton.

5 for a void.

Deduct 1 point when holding only three trumps.

Deduct 1 point for 4-3-3-3 distribution.

"Promote" honors in partner's suit by adding 1 point for the king, queen or jack, but only when the trump holding does not already contain more than 3 points.

Partnership point-count requirements

To make game or slam, it is reckoned that the following points are required:

> Game at no trump or in a major suit, 26 points
>
> Game in a minor suit, 29 points
>
> Small slam, 33 points
>
> Grand slam, 37 points

Requirements for opening the bidding

For opening no-trump bids, see *One No-Trump Opening*, *Two-No Trump Opening* and *Three No-Trump Opening*. For opening bids in a suit:

> 14 points, the hand must be opened
>
> 13 points, an optional opening
>
> 12 points with a good rebid and two quick tricks may be opened
>
> 25 points and a good five-card suit, bid two of the suit
>
> 23 points and a good six-card suit, bid two of the suit
>
> 21 points and good seven-card suit, bid two of the suit

Responding in partner's suit

> Raise to two with 6 to 10 points and trump support
>
> Jump-raise with 13 to 16 points and trump support

Responding in new suit

A minimum of 6 points is required for a new suit at the one-level

A minimum of 10 points is required for a new suit at the two-level

With 19 points, a jump-shift is made.

GOREN SYSTEM

The standard bidding methods described in this book for the most part correspond to the teachings of Charles Goren. His use of the distributional point-count and his theory of no-trump bidding can be found under the appropriate headings.

The main difference between Goren and most modern systems is that Goren has remained faithful to the forcing two-opening, whereas most tournament players nowadays have increased the armory of strong openings by making either two clubs or one club an artificial bid. In conjunction with these, it is usual to play weak major suit two-bids and to assign a special use to two diamonds. There is also a movement away from the forcing double raise of the Goren and Culbertson systems.

GRAND COUP

This is a trump coup with an extra touch of drama. When declarer is reducing his trump length to prepare for the characteristic end position, the cards that he ruffs are winners.

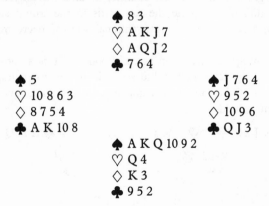

Against four spades the defenders cash three club tricks and switch to a diamond, which South wins in hand.

South plays the ace and king of trump and when West shows out he has to execute a trump coup. In this instance, that involves ruffing two of dummy's red suit winners and being in dummy at the eleventh trick, with these cards remaining:

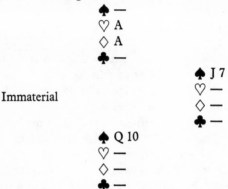

```
              ♠ —
              ♡ A
              ◇ A
              ♣ —
                              ♠ J 7
                              ♡ —
Immaterial                    ◇ —
                              ♣ —
              ♠ Q 10
              ♡ —
              ◇ —
              ♣ —
```

Dummy leads either card and declarer, in effect, finesses against East in the trump suit. That is the characteristic ending of the trump coup. The fact that declarer had to ruff winners to bring about this ending makes it a grand coup: in fact, a double grand coup, since two winners were ruffed. It is possible to construct a quadruple grand coup.

See also *Trump Coup*.

GRAND SLAM FORCE

When a grand slam at a suit contract is under investigation it is sometimes difficult to locate the top cards in the trump suit. The grand slam force provides a conventional way of overcoming that difficulty.

When a trump suit has been agreed upon, 5 NT is a conventional bid requiring the responder to bid seven in the agreed trump suit if he holds two of the top three trump honors (ace, king, queen). For example South holds:

```
    ♠ K J x x      ♡ A K x      ◇ —      ♣ A K Q 10 x x
            South                     North
             2♣                        2♠
              ?
```

Playing the grand slam force, South calls 5 NT, agreeing the spades by inference. Holding the ace and queen of spades, North would call the grand slam. Missing one of these honors, he would respond six spades.

If the partnership is playing a 4 NT convention, such as Blackwood, the grand slam force cannot be used after the conventional 4 NT. For example:

South	North
2♠	4♠
4 NT (Blackwood)	5◇
5 NT	

5 NT is Blackwood, asking for kings. Thus, the grand slam force is useful mainly when the side-suit controls are all in one hand or when they can be located by cue-bids.

Other grand slam tries

There are other, less arbitrary, ways of approaching a grand slam. Any bid of a new suit in between 5 NT and six of the agreed trump suit must logically be a try for seven.

A method called the Baron grand slam try (see *Baron System*) is worth noting, as it allows scope for judgment. When a trump suit has been agreed, and the side-suit controls are accounted for, a bid of six in the suit below the agreed trump suit is a grand slam try. It asks the responder to call the grand slam if his trumps are good. The responder has to exercise his judgment, deciding whether or not his trumps are better than he has already promised. For example, South holds:

♠ Q 10 x   ♡ x x   ◇ A K J x x   ♣ x x x

South	North
—	2♠
3◇	3♡
3♠	4♣ (cue-bid)
4◇ (cue-bid)	6♡ (grand slam try)
?	

Spades are the agreed suit. South might have called the same way with the club queen instead of the spade queen. South's trumps are good, under the circumstances, and he should call seven spades.

GUARD SQUEEZE

This is a squeeze in which one defender has to protect the other from a possible finesse.

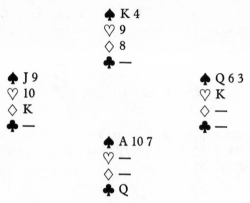

♠ K 4
♡ 9
◇ 8
♣ —

♠ J 9   ♠ Q 6 3
♡ 10   ♡ K
◇ K   ◇ —
♣ —   ♣ —

♠ A 10 7
♡ —
◇ —
♣ Q

South leads the queen of clubs and among the pressures to which West is subjected is the need to protect his partner from a finesse in spades. For the moment West can let go the ten of hearts. Then dummy throws the eight of diamonds and East is squeezed in spades and hearts.

It will be noted that the nine of hearts is a one-card threat controlled by both opponents, yet it is an essential part of the squeeze. That is a characteristic of the guard squeeze. In all other squeeze positions a one-card threat which both opponents control is of no value against best defense.

HERBERT CONVENTION

This convention was originally devised by the Austrian expert, Walter Herbert. It describes the Vienna method of using the bid in the next higher-ranking suit as the negative response to a demand bid. For example:

South	*North*
1♣	1◇ (Herbert)

One club is forcing for one round in the Vienna system. One diamond is the Herbert negative bid, showing less than 8 points (12 Vienna points). Similarly:

South	West	North	East
Pass	1♡	Double	Pass
1♠ (Herbert)			

Vienna uses the Herbert Convention in this situation too. South's one spade bears no relation to his holding in that suit: it merely denies possession of 8 points.

Many forcing-two players adopted Herbert responses to an opening two-bid so that after a sequence such as two diamonds-two hearts (Herbert) the strong hand could bid no trump.

By an extension of meaning, the term Herbert is often applied to any artificial bid in the next higher-ranking suit. In the Fishbein Convention, for example, a bid of the next higher-ranking suit over an opponent's pre-emptive opening is an artificial request for a take-out:

South	West	North	East
Pass	Pass	3♢	3♡ (Fishbein)

Three hearts is a request for a take-out. It is based on the same idea as the Herbert Convention and many European players call it by that name.

HIGH-LOW

This is a method of signaling in which a defender plays a higher card first, then a lower one, to ask that a suit be led or continued. See *Echo.*

HOLD-UP PLAY

A player is said to hold up when for tactical reasons he declines to play a winning card. Usually, his object is to destroy communication between the enemy hands, but there can be other and more subtle reasons for the hold-up.

Here is a simple hold-up to cut communication:

x x

K Q J x x   x x x

A x x

At no trump declarer holds up the ace until the third round. If the

81

lead is subsequently won by East he will have no card of the suit to
return to his partner.

A declarer who has a double guard in the opponents' suit may also
have to hold up.

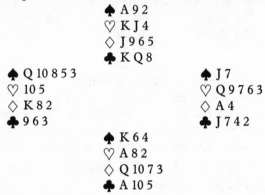

♠ A 9 2
♥ K J 4
♦ J 9 6 5
♣ K Q 8

♠ Q 10 8 5 3   ♠ J 7
♥ 10 5   ♥ Q 9 7 6 3
♦ K 8 2   ♦ A 4
♣ 9 6 3   ♣ J 7 4 2

♠ K 6 4
♥ A 8 2
♦ Q 10 7 3
♣ A 10 5

West leads the five of spades against 3 NT, dummy plays low and East
plays the jack. If declarer wins with the king and tries to establish his
diamond tricks, East will win and the second spade guard will be
removed while West still has the king of diamonds.

Holding up the spade at trick one, declarer is completely safe unless
a defender with five spades holds both ace and king of diamonds.

Hold-up play is equally common in defense. Suppose that when the
suit below is led at no trump there is one side entry to dummy, an entry
that the defenders cannot force out.

Q J 10 x x x

A x   K x x

x x

When South plays small to the queen, both defenders must hold up:
then the suit can never be brought home.

In many cases Hold-up and Ducking are alternative names for the
same maneuver. Under *Ducking* an example is given of a duck by a
defender who wants to give his partner a ruff later on. This is the other
side of the picture:

82

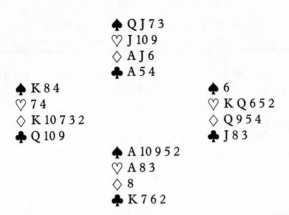

       ♠ Q J 7 3
       ♡ J 10 9
       ◇ A J 6
       ♣ A 5 4

♠ K 8 4   ♠ 6
♡ 7 4   ♡ K Q 6 5 2
◇ K 10 7 3 2   ◇ Q 9 5 4
♣ Q 10 9   ♣ J 8 3

       ♠ A 10 9 5 2
       ♡ A 8 3
       ◇ 8
       ♣ K 7 6 2

Defending against four spades, West leads the seven of hearts and
East plays the queen. If declarer takes the trick, West will come in with
the king of trump and get a heart ruff.

If, on the other hand, declarer reads West for a doubleton heart he
should hold up the ace, destroying the defenders' communication.

Alter the heart position a little and the hold-up is still necessary:

J 10 x

x x x   K Q 9 x

A x x

West leads a heart as before, dummy plays the ten and East the
queen. Reading East for K Q, South holds up the ace. Then East
cannot continue the suit without conceding a second trick.

Hold-up for other tactical reasons

As was mentioned earlier, there are also hold-up plays that are not
primarily concerned with communication. The following is a standard
example:

K Q 10 x

J x x   A 9 x

x x x

South leads small to dummy's king and East holds up; when South leads a second round of the suit he does not know whether to put on the queen or the ten.

Clearly, if East fails to hold up the ace on the first round South will take a winning finesse on the second round (unless he decides arbitrarily to play East for A J alone). A host of more advanced plays are based on the same idea as that.

Some of the most important hold-up plays are those that involve the trump suit (see *Trump Control*). This is an example:

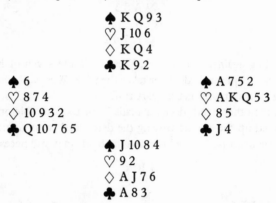

♠ K Q 9 3
♡ J 10 6
◇ K Q 4
♣ K 9 2

♠ 6   ♠ A 7 5 2
♡ 8 7 4   ♡ A K Q 5 3
◇ 10 9 3 2   ◇ 8 5
♣ Q 10 7 6 5   ♣ J 4

♠ J 10 8 4
♡ 9 2
◇ A J 7 6
♣ A 8 3

South plays in four spades and the defenders begin with three rounds of hearts. South ruffs and leads trumps.

Now East must hold up his ace for two rounds. If declarer plays a third round, East wins and plays another round of hearts, forcing North's last trump and setting the contract two tricks. Declarer's best plan is to cut his losses, abandoning trumps and playing on his side suits. East eventually makes his small trump for a one-trick set.

IMMEDIATE OVERCALL

See *Cue-Bid in the Opponents' Suit*.

INVERTED MINOR SUIT RAISES

This means, in effect, that a single raise in a minor is played as stronger than a double raise. Constructively, there is some advantage in playing one diamond—two diamonds as fairly strong, and on a weak distributional hand the double raise has some pre-emptive value. In

Kaplan-Sheinwold the single raise is forcing and has almost no upper limit.

JACOBY TRANSFER BIDS

Jacoby Transfer Bids, suggested by Oswald Jacoby, extend the principle of the Texas Convention to lower levels of bidding. The responder to a 1 NT opener who wishes to play at two of a major bids two of the next lower ranking suit. Opener then bids the suit above and becomes declarer, with the advantage that the lead comes up to the strong hand.

Thus, in the following sequence, North's two heart response requests South to call two spades:

South	*North*
1 NT	2♡

In the same way, a two diamond response to 1 NT would ask partner to call two hearts. The transfer request applies only to major suits and is useful when responder wishes to go no higher than two of a major.

Jacoby draws attention to an important consequence of using the Texas bid at the two-level. The responder gains an extra round of bidding because his partner is compelled to speak again. This extra round of bidding can be exploited where the responder has a long major suit and his values, while not justifying a constructive bid, suggest some possibility of game.

♠ Q x x x x x   ♡ x x   ◇ K J x   ♣ x x

Opposite a strong 1 NT opening, this sort of hand is difficult to judge. A sign-off in two spades is unenterprising, but a jump to four spades may be too much. Jacoby's method provides an answer. First a bid of two hearts asks partner to call two spades. Then three spades invites a game.

In effect, the Jacoby method allows the responder to 1 NT to make a delayed limit call of three in a major, a call that is not available under standard methods, though negotiable in some variations of the Stayman Convention.

JACOBY TWO-BIDS

Jacoby two-bids distinguish between various types of game-going hands. They can be used with any approach-forcing system.

An opening bid of two diamonds, two hearts, or two spades, is game-forcing and promises a very strong holding in the suit named. It also guarantees a singleton or void elsewhere in the hand.

An opening bid of two clubs shows a hand that falls within one of the following categories:

(a) A balanced hand of about 23 points or more, on which the rebid will be no trump.

(b) A game-forcing hand in diamonds, hearts or spades, but without an outside singleton or void.

(c) A game-forcing hand with a strong club suit.

JETTISON SQUEEZE

This is a type of squeeze that is more often found in problems than in actual play, for it depends on a blocked situation which a declarer can generally circumvent at the table.

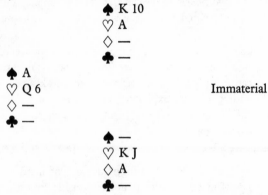

With three cards remaining, South has three winners but cannot run them because of the block in hearts. On the lead of the ace of diamonds, however, West has to let go a heart. Then dummy's ace of hearts is jettisoned and South makes the last two tricks.

JUMP OVERCALL

A jump overcall is a suit overcall one trick higher than the minimum level. For example:

South	West	North	East
1◇	2♡ (or 3♣)		

The usual practice both in Goren and modern American systems is to treat the overcall as weak (see *Weak Jump Overcall*). In the Culbertson system and in Acol the overcall is strong but not forcing. See also *Roman Jump Overcall*.

JUMP PREFERENCE

When the opener has bid two suits and the responder returns to the first suit at a range one higher than necessary, the responder is said to give jump preference. For example:

South	North
1♠	2♣
2♡	3♠

The jump preference is forcing in standard practice. The only time it is not forcing is when responder has limited his hand by an original pass or by a previous bid, as in this sequence:

South	North
1♡	1 NT
2◇	3♡

North's 1 NT limited his hand, so the jump-preference to three hearts can be passed.

JUMP REBID

When the opening bidder, in face of a simple response, rebids his suit at the three-level, that is called a jump rebid. For example:

South	North
1◇	1♠
3◇	

South	North
1♠	1 NT
3♠	

South	North
1♡	2♣
3♡	

In each case South's second call is a jump rebid. (If South were to jump in a new suit that would be a jump-shift, not a jump rebid.)

When the jump rebid follows a response at the one-level, as in the first two examples above, it is strongly invitational but not forcing. A typical hand would contain a good six-card suit and better than minimum strength, usually amounting to about seven playing tricks.

After a response at the two-level, as in the third example above, many American experts treat the jump rebid as forcing. Since the two-level response promises fair values they hold that it is unrealistic to suppose that partner would want to pass the strong rebid.

JUMP-SHIFT

A jump-shift is a change of suit combined with a single jump. The following are examples:

South	North
1♡	2♠

South	North
1♠	3♢

South	North
1♢	1♠
3♣	

South	North
1♡	1♠
2♣	3♢

These jump bids in a new suit are all unconditionally forcing to game in standard practice.

The strength required for a jump-shift on the first round, as in the first two examples above, varies according to distribution and high-card points. Goren's standard is 19 points, and the hand will usually include either a self-supporting suit or strong support for partner.

For a jump-shift on the second round, as in the third example above, the opener needs a hand that will produce a game opposite a bare minimum response. A count of 21 is about the minimum.

Some modern systems, such as Bulldog and Roth-Stone, use weak jump-shift responses. In Kaplan-Sheinwold jump-shifts by the defending side are pre-emptive.

Jump-shift by a passed hand

This is treated as a one-round force, suggesting a maximum pass and usually a fit in opener's suit. In the Acol system there is definite promise of support for partner's major suit, and the opener is expected to bid game in his suit unless completely minimum. This method affords some protection for weak third-hand openings.

KAPLAN-SHEINWOLD SYSTEM

This is one of a group of modern American systems that impose certain artificial techniques on standard approach-forcing methods. Its authors are Alfred Sheinwold and Edgar Kaplan and the principal distinctive features are as follows:

1 NT opening is weak, whether vulnerable or not. In general, all fairly balanced hands of 12 to 14 points are opened 1 NT, but a pass is recommended if the hand does not contain a reasonable quota of quick tricks. The following hand, for example, would not be opened:

$\spadesuit$ Q x x $\heartsuit$ K J x x $\diamondsuit$ Q J x $\clubsuit$ K J x

Lacking a rebiddable major suit, 1 NT may be opened on 5-3-3-2 distribution or even, exceptionally, 5-4-2-2 distribution.

The Stayman Convention may be used in responding to a 1 NT opening. Other responses are normal, except three clubs and three diamonds, which are pre-emptive bids.

Major-suit openings guarantee a five-card suit.

A response of 1 NT is forcing for one round but denies the ability to make a constructive bid. It may contain from 5 to 11 points and it also has a wide distributional range.

A 1 NT response may be given on the sort of hand that is worth a limit-raise to three of the major suit. On the next round, the responder shows his hand by raising to three. Otherwise, immediate raises of a major-suit opening are mainly in accordance with Standard American.

A rebid of 1 NT by the opening bidder promises a balanced hand with 15 to 17 points. Thus:

South	North
1 $\diamondsuit$	1 $\spadesuit$
1 NT	

If responder now bids a new suit over 1 NT that is forcing.

A single raise of a minor-suit opening is forcing and denies a four-card major. The minimum strength is 9 points and there is no maximum.

A double raise of a minor-suit opening is weak.

Two-level responses to partner's suit opening promise that the responder will bid again on the second round. Thus, although not game-forcing by definition, these responses become nearly so in practice.

Weak two-bids are used. Two clubs is the only forcing opening.

Jump overcalls are weak.

Jump-shift responses are weak if made in competition. For example:

South	West	North	East
Pass	1♣	1♠	3◇

After North's overcall East's jump-shift is weak, based on a long suit with few points.

A jump-shift response is also weak if partner is the overcaller:

South	West	North	East
1♡	2♣	Pass	3♠

East's three spades is weak, as in the preceding example.

Psychic openings are of the "controlled" variety. They are made preferably on a five-card suit headed by the ace, king or queen. The total strength of the hand should range from 3 to 6 points and there must be no ace or king in a side suit.

A psychic opener normally passes any response other than a jump-shift. In response to a jump-shift he discloses a psychic by rebidding his suit or by bidding 2 NT, whichever is the cheaper.

KOCK-WERNER REDOUBLE

This convention, which is associated with the names of two Swedish players, extends the use of S.O.S. redoubles to many situations in which a redouble, according to standard methods, would show strength. The principle is that when partner's overcall at the range of one or two has been doubled for penalties a redouble should be an alarm-signal calling upon the overcaller to find some other resting place.

South	West	North	East
1♡	1♠	Double	Redouble

South	West	North	East
1♡	Pass	1 NT	Pass
Pass	2♣	Double	Redouble

In both sequences the redouble asks West to transfer to one of the other suits, including the suit (or it may be suits) bid by the enemy. When a defensive pair is on the run it quite ofteri happens that a suit bid by the enemy is the best resting place. One of the advantages of the Kock-Werner Convention is that it makes it easier for that haven to be found.

LANDY CONVENTION

This method of competing against an opponent's 1 NT opening was devised by Alvin Landy of New York. An overcall of two clubs, either by second or fourth player, is used as a form of take-out double, with good preparedness for both major suits. Vulnerability and the strength of the opponent's no-trump are important factors, but in general the overcall is competitive rather than constructive.

Since a responder with a club suit can pass the artificial bid, it is possible to make a response of three clubs conventional, asking the Landy overcaller to name his longer or better major.

LAVINTHAL

The method of signaling first suggested by the American player, Hy Lavinthal, is discussed under *Suit-Preference Signal*.

LEAD AGAINST NO-TRUMP

In so far as a general distinction can be made between leads against no trump and against a suit, the lead against no trump is intended to attack rather than to play safe. The best attack usually lies in the longest and strongest suit, and for the most part it is in order to lead from that suit.

Fourth best lead

According to an old and well-founded convention, the fourth best card is led from a long suit. From K J 8 6 the six is led and from A Q 8 5 2 the five is led. For examples of the deductions that can be drawn from this lead, see *Rule of Eleven*.

The lead from a suit headed by three honors

There are some exceptions to the practice of leading fourth best. When three honors are held, the conventional lead is the higher of touching honors. From K Q J the king is led, from A Q J the queen, from A J 10 and K J 10 the jack. The king is often led from K Q 9 as well as from K Q 10.

From A K Q and A K J the king is usually led; from A K 10 x the king may be led, but from a longer suit the fourth best. From A Q 10 fourth best is normal, but when a sure side entry is held the ace may be preferred.

The lead from a broken sequence

The queen is usual from a suit headed by Q J 9, the jack from J 10 8, the 10 from 10 9 7.

The lead from an inner sequence

From suits headed by A 10 9, K 10 9 and Q 10 9, the ten is the conventional lead. With a five-card suit, however, it may be impolitic to expend an honor, and players often lead fourth best.

The lead of an ace

By tradition, the lead of an ace is a command to partner to drop his highest card unless it is evident that such play would cost a trick. The purpose is partly to discover the lie and partly to allow a player to run his long suit without being blocked by his partner, but it must be said that the need for this convention does not often arise and some partnerships have abandoned it.

The lead in a suit bid by partner

The higher card is always led from a doubleton. From three low cards, such as 7 5 2, the top card is traditional, but many modern players, in this and similar situations, lead the 5 and follow with the 7. This method is known colloquially as MUD (Middle, Up, Down).

From three cards headed by an honor the lowest card is led. The lead
of the honor would give away a trick in a position such as the following:

6 3

Q 9 4   K 10 8 5 2

A J 7

With J x x and 10 x x there is the additional point that when dummy
has a singleton or doubleton honor the high card often cannot be
spared. For example:

J 4

10 6 2   K Q 8 7 5

A 9 3

The lead of the ten would cost a trick.

From three cards headed by touching honors, such as J 10 x, the top
card is led. When non-touching honors are held, such as K J x or
A 10 x, the low card is conventionally correct and will sometimes save
a trick, but the player must bear in mind the danger that the suit may
become blocked for the defense.

From four cards the lead is mostly the same as if the player were
leading his own long suit; but the king would be led from K Q x x,
and from a holding such as Q J 8 2 the queen rather than the two would
be advisable, because of the danger that the suit might become blocked.

The lead of a short suit

When leading from a short suit that has not been bid, the usual
practice is to lead the higher card from a doubleton and either the
middle or the lowest from three cards.

See also *Rusinow Lead* and *Top of Nothing Lead*.

LEAD AGAINST TRUMP CONTRACT

When leading against a trump contract a player does not set out to establish long suits in the way that he does at no trump. When he wants to attack he is more likely to lead from a short suit. More often, however, the paramount consideration is safety—a lead that may turn out to be constructive and meanwhile will not give a trick away.

Short suit leads

A lead from a singleton or a doubleton or three small is common. The higher card is led from a doubleton.

From x x x the modern tendency is to lead the middle card and follow with the top card. See *Lead against No Trump*.

Leading from honors

The top card is usually led from touching honors, even when there are only two high cards in sequence, as with K Q x x or Q J x x. From J 10 x x sometimes the jack is led, sometimes fourth best.

From three cards headed by an unsupported honor other than the ace, the lowest card is usual. From a suit headed by the ace the conventional lead is the ace, but a low card has deceptive value and is sometimes preferred when it is unlikely that any player has a singleton in the suit.

The traditional lead from a combination headed by A K or A K Q is the king, but many tournament players, especially in Europe, lead the ace, in conformity with the general practice of leading the top card from a sequence.

To show a doubleton A K, normal practice is reversed: players who lead the king from A K x now lead the ace.

From a long suit not headed by the ace or by one of the honor combinations mentioned above, fourth best is normal; but when the suit contains no honor a top or middle card will often be preferred.

Forcing leads

When a defender has length in trumps, or judges that his partner may have length, he has to give thought to an attacking lead that may cause declarer to lose control of the trump suit by forcing him to ruff (see *Forcing Tactics*). The bidding is a player's best guide in this respect.

Suppose that the defender holds the following and the contract is four spades:

♠ 9 6 5 3
♡ K 10 8 6 4
♢ 5
♣ K 8 3

If the bidding has been one spade—four spades, there will be no advantage in forcing declarer to ruff, for dummy surely has four trumps; dummy, therefore, will retain trump control even if declarer loses it. The singleton diamond is the most likely-looking lead.

If the bidding were one diamond (from the eventual dummy)—two spades; three diamonds—four spades, then it would be best to look for tricks in clubs, for declarer's trump holding would probably be unassailable.

But if the bidding went in a way that suggested five trumps in declarer's hand and two or three in dummy's, then a forcing lead, designed to deplete declarer's trump reserve, would be indicated. On the hand above, the fourth best heart would be chosen.

Trump leads

A trump lead may be chosen for safety or to forestall a ruffing game or to prevent declarer from making small trumps when a defender has greater length. A trump lead is generally in order when partner has made a penalty pass of a take-out double (see *Penalty Pass*).

Technically, it is hardly ever wrong to lead the lowest trump, but most players lead the top card from two, the lowest from three.

LEAD-DIRECTING DOUBLE

A double whose main object is to inspire a killing lead is called a lead-directing double. The Lightner slam double is the best known example, but lead-directing doubles of no-trump contracts and cue-bids can also be made.

Double of no-trump

A double of no trump can be recognized as lead-directing when there is a surprise element about it: when it can be judged that the player cannot have doubled on all-round strength. For example:

South	West	North	East
Pass	Pass	1♡	Pass
2 NT	Pass	Pass	Double

Since East has not bid over one heart, but has made a non-free double of 2 NT, it is clear that something is afoot: East has strength in hearts and wants a heart lead.

South	West	North	East
Pass	Pass	1♡	Pass
2♢	Pass	2 NT	Pass
3 NT	Double		

Here, West has doubled 3 NT although he passed originally and his partner has not spoken. The only explanation is that he urgently requires a diamond lead.

The following general rules apply to lead-directing doubles, in order of priority:

(a) When the doubler has bid a suit, the double confirms that he wants that suit to be led.

(b) When the doubler's partner has bid a suit, the double recommends a lead of that suit.

(c) When the doubling side has not entered the auction, as in the examples above, the double usually directs attention to the first suit bid by dummy.

Double of cue-bids

Opportunities for lead-directing doubles may arise when the opponents are making cue-bids (responses to Blackwood, for instance). Equally, negative inferences may be drawn from a player's failure to double a cue-bid. The inference will be that the lead of another suit is preferred.

LEAD-INHIBITING BIDS

These are tactical bids, in the nature of mild psychic bids, which are designed to prevent a damaging lead. For example:

♠ K J x   ♡ K J x   ◊ A x x   ♣ Q 10 x x

The natural way of calling this hand is to open one club and to rebid

1 NT over a simple suit response. An opening of one diamond, made with the idea of discouraging a diamond lead against a no-trump contract, would be a lead-inhibiting bid.

Lead-inhibiting bids can equally be made by responder on this type of hand:

♠ K x x x x   ♡ —   ◇ A K x x x x   ♣ x x

Partner opens one spade and responder bids two clubs.

The bid can also be made at a higher level, as a false cue-bid.

LIGHTNER SLAM DOUBLE

This convention was first proposed by Theodore Lightner and has been adopted universally by good players.

It is based on the idea that a player seldom wants to double a slam contract merely to increase the penalty (unless, of course, it is an obvious sacrifice), so that the double is more usefully employed to indicate the best defense to a slam.

Primarily, the Lightner double asks for an unusual or unexpected lead. It is often made by a player who has a void suit or who has tricks in a suit called by the opponents. The player on lead must use his judgment in deciding which suit is called for and must give regard to the bidding and to the nature of his own hand.

He should reject a harmless lead, such as a trump, or an obvious lead, such as a suit bid by his own side. He should also reject the unbid suit or suits when it seems that one of those would be the natural lead. In most cases he should give preference to the first side suit bid by dummy, or to a side suit bid by declarer.

It follows that a player should not double a slam if he wishes his partner to make a normal lead. Of course, if he feels sure of defeating the slam no matter what suit is led, he may double just the same.

LIMIT-BID

A limit-bid is one that describes the strength of a player's hand within fairly narrow limits. A player who has made such a bid is said to be "limited."

Thus, an opening bid or response in no trump is a limit-bid, for the requisite strength is closely defined. A response in a new suit, whether a simple response or a jump, is not a limit-bid, for the range of strength can be very wide.

Limit-raise

A raise of partner's suit is generally a limit-raise, expressing the full value of the hand. There are two main exceptions to this rule:

1. A double raise of partner's suit opening is game-forcing in standard practice, except where the responder has previously passed. Many players also treat the double raise in competition as a limit-bid.

2. When a game-forcing situation has been created, a raise of partner's suit is not necessarily a limit-raise. For example:

South	North
1♣	1♡
2♠	3♠

North's three spades does not necessarily express the full value of his hand.

LITTLE MAJOR

This highly complicated system was evolved by Terence Reese and Jeremy Flint of London as a counter to the artificial methods employed by the Italians and other Continental teams. The following are the main opening sequences:

1♣   In principle, a heart suit. One diamond is a negative response but may also be the first move on a big hand. Response of 1 NT is semi-positive, may be balanced, or contain a suit, or support for hearts. Responses of one spade, one club and two diamonds are positive. Responses in hearts are natural raises. Rebids in no-trump indicate various distributional types.

1◇   *Either* a spade suit *or* a strong balanced hand. A rebid in no-trump signifies the balanced hand except when 2 NT is bid after a positive response. One heart is a negative response but may be the first move on a big hand. Positive and semi-positive responses as over one club.

1♡   *Either* very strong *or* quite weak, signified by a pass on the next round. Responses are based on controls.

1♠   A limited opening, about 12-15, with some values in both minor suits and no biddable major. Responses of 1 NT and two diamonds set various conventional sequences in motion.

1 NT   Natural, 14-16. Response of two clubs is Stayman, and two diamonds Gladiator, requiring the opener to rebid two hearts. Many conventional sequences follow.

2♣, 2◇   Limited hand with one fair minor suit, no biddable major, range about 12-15.

2♡, 2♠   Useful major-minor two-suiter. Response of 2 NT introduces various conventional sequences.

2 NT   *Either* a minor suit pre-empt *or* a strong minor two-suiter.

3♣, 3◇   Strong playing values, concentrated in the minors.

3♡, 3♠, 4♡, 4♠ Normal pre-empts.

4♣, 4◇   *Texas* for four hearts and four spades respectively. *Roman Blackwood* is used and various *asking bids*.

Defensive bidding:

Immediate overcalls in opponent's suit show various kinds of distributional hands.

Responses to take-out doubles are mostly made in a short suit.

Aspro (a variation of *Astro*) is used over an opponent's 1 NT.

LOSER-ON-LOSER PLAY

When declarer forbears to ruff a losing card and instead discards a loser of another suit, he is said to play loser-on-loser. This play can be made with tactical advantage in many different situations. A common reason for the play is to preserve the trump holding.

To save a trump trick

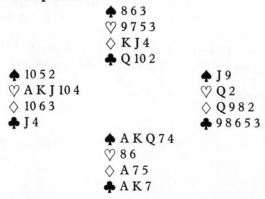

♠ 8 6 3
♡ 9 7 5 3
◇ K J 4
♣ Q 10 2

♠ 10 5 2   ♠ J 9
♡ A K J 10 4   ♡ Q 2
◇ 10 6 3   ◇ Q 9 8 2
♣ J 4   ♣ 9 8 6 5 3

♠ A K Q 7 4
♡ 8 6
◇ A 7 5
♣ A K 7

South is playing four spades and the defense begins with king, ace and jack of hearts. If East ruffs the third heart South must not overruff. If he does, he will lose a trump trick and later a diamond. Instead, South must throw his losing diamond.

To avoid an overruff

When there is a loser to ruff in dummy, but reason to believe that the next defender will overruff, a solution may be to discard a loser in another suit, preparing later to ruff that suit.

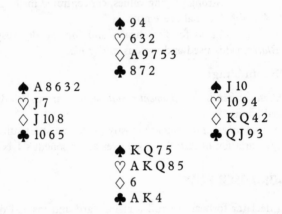

Against four hearts West leads the jack of diamonds, taken by dummy's ace. A spade to the king falls to the ace, and West switches to a trump.

Declarer needs only one ruff from dummy for his tenth trick. However, the fall of East's high spade alerts declarer to the possibility that East may be able to overruff the third round of spades and take out dummy's last trump.

After winning West's trump return at trick three, declarer's best plan is to try a loser-on-loser play. He cashes the top spade and leads the five, but instead of ruffing in dummy he discards a club. Later, he makes his tenth trick by ruffing a club.

Loser-on-loser elimination

Declarer often prepares for an elimination ending by discarding a loser on a loser.

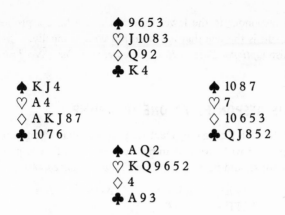

```
                    ♠ 9 6 5 3
                    ♡ J 10 8 3
                    ◇ Q 9 2
                    ♣ K 4
      ♠ K J 4                      ♠ 10 8 7
      ♡ A 4                        ♡ 7
      ◇ A K J 8 7                  ◇ 10 6 5 3
      ♣ 10 7 6                     ♣ Q J 8 5 2
                    ♠ A Q 2
                    ♡ K Q 9 6 5 2
                    ◇ 4
                    ♣ A 9 3
```

West opens one diamond and South eventually reaches four hearts. West leads the king of diamonds and switches to ace and another trump.

Expecting the spade finesse to be wrong, declarer plans an elimination combined with loser-on-loser play. He ruffs dummy's nine of diamonds, plays the king and ace of clubs and enters dummy with a third-round club ruff. Then he leads dummy's queen of diamonds and throws the two of spades. West is in and has to lead a spade or give a ruff and discard.

For other forms of loser-on-loser play, see *Scissors Coup* and *Avoidance Play*.

LOWER MINOR CONVENTION

This is one of the many methods proposed as a defense against enemy three-openings. The convention is that the player should bid the cheaper minor as a request for a take-out.

South	West	North	East
		3♣	3◇

South	West	North	East
3♡	Pass	Pass	4♣

In each case East's bid requests partner to show a suit.

Like the *Fishbein Convention*, this method of defense against three-bids permits Double and 3 NT to be used in their natural sense. Against that, four clubs and three diamonds are not available as natural bids, and the responder to the lower minor call may have a problem when his best suit is the one that has been bid conventionally.

See also *Optional Double, Reese Defense,* and *Three No-Trump Take-out.*

MALTAIS RESPONSES TO ONE NO-TRUMP

R. Maltais of Kenogami, Quebec, proposes that when an opponent has intervened with two of a minor suit over 1 NT, a response in the other minor should be Stayman (see *Stayman Convention*).

	South	West	North	East
(1)	1 NT	2♣	2♦	
(2)	1 NT	2♦	3♣	

In both cases North asks the opener to show length in a major.

When the overcall is in a major suit, three of a minor shows that minor suit and length in the unbid major.

(3)	1 NT	2♡	3♦

North has diamonds and is interested in spades.

Compare *Reese Convention.*

McCABE ADJUNCT

A device to play in three of a new suit after partner has opened with a *Weak Two-Bid.* The responder bids 2 NT, which requires opener to rebid three clubs. If clubs is the responder's suit he passes. If he aims to play in one of the other suits he bids three of that suit, and the opener is expected to pass.

McKENNEY CONVENTION

This name is applied by some players to the method of signaling described under *Suit-Preference Signal.*

MENACE

This is an alternative name for threat—a card that an opponent has to protect in a squeeze position. See *Threat.*

102

MERRIMAC COUP

This is the sacrifice of an unsupported high card with the object of knocking out a vital entry (compare the *Deschapelles Coup*, which is similar). The usual occasion for defense to use the Merrimac Coup is when dummy has a long suit and only one outside entry.

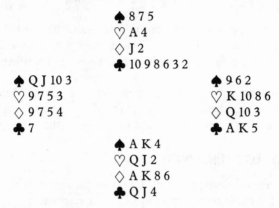

♠ 8 7 5
♡ A 4
◇ J 2
♣ 10 9 8 6 3 2

♠ Q J 10 3   ♠ 9 6 2
♡ 9 7 5 3   ♡ K 10 8 6
◇ 9 7 5 4   ◇ Q 10 3
♣ 7   ♣ A K 5

♠ A K 4
♡ Q J 2
◇ A K 8 6
♣ Q J 4

West leads the queen of spades against 3 NT. South wins and attacks clubs. East ducks the first round of clubs and wins the second, West discarding a heart.

It is clear now that dummy's entry, the ace of hearts, must be removed before the clubs are established. East, therefore, leads the king of hearts, the Merrimac coup. This gives away a sure heart trick but prevents dummy's long suit from being brought in. Careful defense now beats the contract.

MEXICAN TWO DIAMONDS

An artificial two-diamond opening, showing a hand just short of a 2 NT bid, in the 19 to 21 point range. Responder can pass with diamond length or sign off in two hearts or two spades with length in those suits. With a weak balanced hand, the sign-off is 2 NT. Other responses are positive and three clubs is Stayman.

MICHAELS CUE-BID

Like *Astro Cue-Bid* and *Colorful Cue-Bid*, this is an attempt to solve the problem of overcalling on two-suited hands. The proposals of

Mike Michaels of Miami Beach are concerned especially with finding a major-suit contract.

When an opponent has opened with one of a minor, an immediate overcall in the same suit suggests at least nine cards in the major suits and a hand too weak for a take-out double, such as:

♠ K J 8 5 3   ♡ K J 9 2   ◇ 7 2   ♣ 10 6

When the opponents have bid a major suit, the cue-bid must be stronger, for reasons of safety. There is no upper limit and the bid guarantees at least four cards in the unbid major together with one minor suit.

New-suit responses to the Michaels cue-bid are not forcing and responder is expected to bid the limit. With a strong hand but no immediate fit, responder may force by repeating the enemy suit.

MURRAY TWO DIAMONDS

A convention devised by the Canadian international player, Eric Murray, for use in responding to 1 NT. The response simply asks the opener to show his longer major, or to bid two hearts with equal length in both majors. The main value of the convention arises on moderate two-suiters, for the partnership can be assured of landing in the better major-suit part score. At duplicate, especially, this may be important.

NEAPOLITAN SYSTEM

This is one of the principal Italian systems, played by Forquet and Garozzo and others. It is a one-club system, with a series of artificial responses.

A one-club opening shows at least 17 points and probably good distribution as well. The partner responds in terms of "controls." A king counts as one control and an ace as two controls. These are the responses to one club:

No control	One diamond
One control (king)	One heart
Two controls (ace or two kings)	One spade
Three controls (one ace and one king, or three kings)	1 NT
Two clubs shows four controls, two diamonds five controls, and 2 NT	

six controls. The missing bids, two hearts and two spades, are natural and weak.

This system of showing controls is used equally when there has been an intervening bid. Responder passes if he has no control, bids one step higher than the interference bid to show one control, two steps higher to show two controls, and so on.

The Neapolitan system has a number of other specialized bids but, apart from the one-club opening and responses, the general structure of the bidding is natural.

NEGATIVE DOUBLES

Devised by Alvin Roth, of New York City, for use in the Roth-Stone system, this style of double has been adopted by many players of other systems. Extending the principle of the co-operative double, it makes the double of a simple overcall in a suit not a punitive measure but a means of showing a moderate degree of honor strength when no other suitable bid presents itself.

Suppose that the bidding goes:

South	West	North	East
1♣	1♠	?	

North holds any of these hands:

1. ♠ 7 5 3   ♡ K J 7 4   ◇ A 10 8   ♣ J 6 2
2. ♠ A J 8 5 2   ♡ 6 3   ◇ K 9 6 4   ♣ 10 2
3. ♠ 7 4   ♡ A 10 7   ◇ K Q 8 6 3   ♣ 9 6 3

In each example North can double one spade to show that he has a certain measure of strength, about 8 to 10 points.

It will be noted that on the second hand North has a sound penalty double of one spade. But a consequence of using this convention is that a player cannot double for penalties at this point.

On the third hand North has a fair suit and many players would reckon the general strength sufficient for a free bid of two diamonds. In the Roth-Stone system the standard for a free bid, especially in a higher-ranking suit, is unusually high. The negative double fits into the system because it enables the responder to show a moderate degree of strength.

NEGATIVE RESPONSE

This is the usual term for a weakness response to a forcing bid. For example, in reply to a forcing two-opening, 2 NT is the negative response.

The term is used more loosely to describe a weak limited response, such as 1 NT over an opening bid.

NO-TRUMP BIDDING

Standard practice in no-trump openings is discussed under the titles, *One No-Trump Opening*, *Two No-Trump Opening* and *Three No-Trump Opening*.

Other titles concerned with no-trump bidding are: *No-Trump Overcalls*, *No-Trump Responses to Suit Opening*, *Quantitative Four No Trump*, *Stayman Convention* and *Weak No Trump*.

NO-TRUMP OVERCALL

An overcall of 1 NT normally shows similar values to an opening strong no-trump, including a guard in the opponent's suit. The overcall is weaker in the protective situation (see *Protective Bid*).

An overcall of 2 NT is played in different ways. In theory, it is a strong bid based on 22 to 23 points, but it is often made on a somewhat weaker hand with a long minor suit.

See also *Gardener No-Trump Overcall* and *Unusual No-Trump*.

NO-TRUMP RESPONSES TO SUIT OPENING

1 NT response

A response of 1 NT shows a moderate hand in the 6-to-10 point range. It tends to deny a worthwhile suit that can be bid at the one-level.

Over one club the response of 1 NT is somewhat stronger, generally 9-11 points.

For specialized uses of the 1 NT response, see *Kaplan-Sheinwold* and *Roth-Stone System*.

2 NT response

This is game-forcing in standard practice and promises the equivalent of a sound opening bid with balanced distribution, about 13 to 15 points.

Many players, however, follow the style of the *Acol System*, where 2 NT as a natural response on about 11 to 13 points is regarded as a valuable work-horse.

3 NT response

In standard practice this shows the sort of hand that is suitable for a strong 1 NT opening, about 16 to 18 points. For players who treat the response of 2 NT as a limit-bid, 3 NT suggests about 14 to 16.

ONE NO-TRUMP OPENING

An opening bid of 1 NT normally shows a balanced hand with 16 to 18 points, and a guard in at least three suits. Some players use a weak no-trump of about 12 to 14 points when not vulnerable, while others use a weak no-trump throughout (see *Weak No-Trump*).

The responder with a balanced hand raises to 3 NT if he can judge that the partnership holds at least 25 to 26 points in the combined hands. Thus, 9 points opposite a strong 1 NT opening would be enough for a raise to 3 NT. With a little less, the responder would give an invitational raise to 2 NT.

A response of two in a suit is generally played as a sign-off, expressing a desire to play in that spot. A response of three in a suit is game-forcing.

Many conventions have been developed for use by the responder to a 1 NT opening. The most popular is the Stayman convention, designed primarily for the location of major suits. See also *Gerber*, *Gladiator* and *Texas Conventions* and *Jacoby Transfer Bids*.

OPENING SUIT BIDS OF ONE

Opening bids of one of a suit cover a wide range, from 13 to about 21 points.

In standard practice the usual minimum on balanced hands is about

13 points or $2\frac{1}{2}$ to 3 honor-tricks. When there is good distribution the high card requirements can be lowered. Most authorities would consider the following about a minimum for a sound opening:

♠ K J 9 x x x   ♡ Q x x   ♢ A x x   ♣ x

A bid of one on anything less than that comes into the semi-psychic class.

Choice of suits

When there is more than one biddable suit the choice of which to open is a complex subject. The general rules are:

(a) Between five-card suits of equal length, prefer the higher-ranking. Exception: with clubs and spades one club is usually preferred.

(b) Between five- and six-card suits, generally bid the longer, but on moderate hands, prefer the higher-ranking when the suits are adjacent.

(c) Between five- and four-card suits, bid the longer suit first except: when the suits are adjacent, the four-card suit ranks higher and the hand is not strong enough for a reverse. For example:

♠ A x   ♡ x x   ♢ A K J 9   ♣ Q 10 x x x

One diamond is sounder than one club. See *Reverse Bid*.

(d) When only four-card suits are held, the necessity of having a sound rebid has to be studied. On moderate hands the lower suit is generally sounder unless the suits are touching.

When the suits are spades and diamonds, support for the other two suits has to be considered:

♠ K Q x x   ♡ K 10 x   ♢ A Q x x   ♣ x x

One spade is the correct opening, for it leaves a sound rebid over any response at the two-level. If one diamond were opened and partner responded two clubs, there would not be a sound rebid. Change over the hearts and the clubs, and one diamond would be correct.

(e) On 4-4-4-1 hands there is a general rule in favor of bidding the suit below the singleton, in order to facilitate the rebid. The strength of the suits is an important consideration, however. When the short suit is diamonds and both majors are biddable, one spade is generally a better opening than one club.

Short suit openings

It is common practice to open a three-card club suit on certain types of balanced hands (see *Short Club*). Some players extend that practice, on occasion, to three-card diamond suits.

See also *Third Hand Opening* and *Fourth Hand Opening*.

OPTIMUM STRATEGY

The term relates to a defender's duty to vary his play with certain holdings. Take this familiar position:

A J 9 x

Q 10 x   K x x

x x x

The declarer's best chance of developing the maximum number of tricks is to play West for Q 10 x or K 10 x. He leads low, intending to finesse the nine and to take a second finesse later if the nine fetches a high honor.

To counter this play, the regulation strategy for West is to play a high honor from Q 10 x or K 10 x. Declarer will then have a more open guess on the next round. Similarly, with K Q x, West will normally play low, expecting declarer to put in the nine.

Against a defender who always plays in this fashion, however, declarer can re-establish his advantage. When West plays low, South will know that the nine cannot gain and will finesse the jack, winning the extra trick when West has K Q x.

The defender must vary his play, therefore, sometimes putting in the queen, sometimes playing low.

OPTIONAL DOUBLE

An optional double is one that leaves partner with an open choice, whether to take out the double or pass for penalties.

By partnership arrangement, the optional double can be used when there has been an adverse pre-emptive opening. Used in that way, it promises support for partner if he elects to take out the double, and fair defensive values if he leaves the double in for penalties. It does not promise strength in the opponent's suit.

The following hand would be suitable for an optional double of an enemy three-heart opening:

♠ A J x x ♡ x ◇ K J x x ♣ A K x x

As the example suggests, the optional double of a three-bid is closer to a take-out than a penalty double. For other defensive methods see *Fishbein Convention, Lower Minor Convention, Reese Defense,* and *Three No-Trump Take-out.*

Double of 1 NT

A double of a one no-trump opening is primarily for penalties, but is optional to the extent that partner may take out if his hand is unsuitable for defense.

OUT-OF-THE-BLUE CUE-BID

This term is used in Britain to describe a special form of *Advance Cue-Bid.*

(1)	South	North	(2)	South	North
	1♡	1♠		1◇	1♡
	4◇			1♠	4♣

These jumps have no natural meaning, for a bid at a lower level would be forcing. They are used to confirm partner's last-named suit and to indicate first-round control of the suit in which the jump is made.

For different interpretations of the same kind of sequence, see *Fragment Bid* and *Void-Showing Bid.*

Other situations in which the double may be said to be optional in character are dealt with under *Co-operative Double.*

OVERCALL

An overcall is a bid made after an opponent has opened the bidding. If made at the minimum level it is a simple, as opposed to a jump, overcall. For example:

(See hand on next page.)

South	West	North	East
		1♣	1♠

South	West	North	East
1◇	Pass	1 NT	2♡

There is no fixed standard in terms of point-count for simple over-calls. Playing strength is the main consideration (see *Rule of Two and Three*). The following would be a reasonable, but minimum, overcall of one spade, non-vulnerable:

♠ K Q J x x   ♡ x x   ◇ x x x   ♣ K 10 x

On strong hands other measures are available: see *Cue-Bid in Opponents' Suit, Jump Overcall, No-Trump Overcalls, Take-out Double*. For overcalls in a protective situation, see *Protective Bid*.

Responding to overcalls

A player who has made an overcall on a moderate hand is not obliged to rebid over a simple response.

South	West	North	East
1♣	1♠	Pass	2◇

East's two diamonds is non-forcing. A jump-shift (three diamonds, for example) would be forcing for one round.

A double raise of an overcall is also non-forcing.

OVERTAKING SQUEEZE

This is a rare position in which there must be trumps in both hands when the squeeze begins.

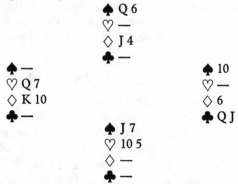

Playing in spades, South cannot cross-ruff the last four tricks because East will overruff dummy. South, therefore, leads the jack of spades and, depending on which suit West unguards, overtakes or not with dummy's queen of spades.

PART-SCORE BIDDING

Bids that would ordinarily be forcing to game are treated as forcing for at least one round when, owing to a part score, they are already enough for game. For instance, playing the forcing two, an opening bid of two hearts at 60 on score is still forcing. At the same score, a response of two spades to partner's one-diamond opening would be forcing for at least one round.

The main effect of a part score on bidding tactics is that both sides will strive to get into the bidding early. From a part score of 60 or more, many hands are opened one spade or 1 NT (even slightly under strength) that otherwise would be opened, if at all, with an approach-bid in a minor suit. Equally, when it is the opponents who have the part score, aggressive action is generally the best.

PASSED HAND

A passed hand is one that failed to bid on the first round. Responses by a passed hand differ from first-round responses. Whereas a simple response in a new suit by a player who has not passed is forcing for one round (see *Responses to Opening Bids*), a simple take-out by a passed hand is not forcing, even for one round, in standard practice. This has a bearing on the choice of response to partner's third- or fourth-hand opening. For example, North deals and opens one spade and South holds the following:

♠ K 8 3   ♥ A 9 7 2   ♦ 6 4   ♣ A 6 3 2

South should make a temporizing bid of two clubs. If South were a passed hand, however, that bid would be inadvisable on such a weak suit; North, not being obliged to keep the bidding open, might pass. Three spades would be a better bid despite the lack of four-card support.

A jump-shift by a passed hand is treated as forcing for one round and is generally based on a maximum pass and a fit in the opener's suit.

See also *Drury Convention* and *Jump-shift*.

PENALTY DOUBLE

This is a business double as distinct from an optional double or a take-out double. The rules for recognizing a request for a take-out are described under *Take-Out Double*.

A double after partner has entered the auction is always a penalty double, unless the partnership has agreed to use the responsive double or negative double in certain special situations. These conventions are described separately.

A double of an opponent's 1 NT opening is also primarily for penalties. As always, however, the partner may take out the double if his hand is unsuitable.

There are some situations where a double that is, by definition, a penalty double should nevertheless be taken out by the partner unless his hand is reasonably well suited to defense (see *Co-operative Double*). On the other hand, there are cases where a player converts a take-out double into a double for penalties (see *Penalty Pass*).

Doubles of high calls

A double of 2 NT is always for penalties. A double of an opponent's pre-emptive opening at the range of two or three depends on partnership style. If the optional double is not played, and if there is a conventional bid for a take-out, such as Fishbein or 3 NT, then a double will be for penalties.

A double of a four-level opening is for penalties but generally promises honor-tricks as well as trump strength. Thus partner can take out the double at his discretion.

Mathematics of the penalty double

In all close situations the odds are weighted against the doubler to a much greater extent than most players realize. For example, a double of a major-suit game when declarer is not vulnerable will cost 170 points if the contract is just made and is not redoubled. But one down will bring in only an extra 50 points, so the doubler is laying odds of nearly 7 to 2. When declarer is vulnerable the odds are not so unfavorable.

In rubber bridge, the loss from doubling non-vulnerable opponents into game, as compared with the extra points gained when they go down one, is 7 to 1; when they are vulnerable, 5 to 1. (The figure, 7 to 1, is reached as follows: the double, if unsuccessful, will add about 70 for tricks plus 50 bonus plus 300 game equity; from this must be subtracted about 70 part score equity since, if doubled out, opponents will not have a part score; making a total of 350 points as against an additional 50 in penalties.)

PENALTY PASS

This occurs when a player decides to pass his partner's take-out double. For example:

South	West	North	East
1♡	Double	Pass	Pass

West's double is for a take-out and East's pass is a penalty pass. East's hand will be of the following kind:

♠ x x   ♡ Q J 10 9 x x   ◇ A x x   ♣ x x

A player who makes a penalty pass when sitting under the bidder will always have length and strength in the trump suit. In general, therefore, it will be sound play for the doubler to lead a trump.

In the following example, the player who passes for penalties is sitting over the opponent's call:

South	West	North	East
1♡	Pass	Pass	Double
Pass	Pass		

Sitting over the heart bidder, West does not have to be so strong in hearts to make a penalty pass.

POINT-COUNT

The simplest way of measuring the strength of a hand is by allocating a point-value to each honor card. The strength needed for various opening bids and responses can then be stated in terms of points. Most systems use the point-count of 4-3-2-1, for A K Q J respectively, first popularized by Milton Work.

This count was originally applied to no-trump bidding only, but Goren and others extended the method to suit contracts, counting points for long suits and for ruffing values. An adjusted point-count of that kind is called a distributional point-count. See *Goren Point-Count.*

Other systems, such as Acol, retain the point-count for no-trump bidding but do not use any such method of valuation for suit contracts.

114

It is generally reckoned that 3 NT is worth bidding on a combined 25 to 26 count. For 6 NT, in the absence of long suits, about 33 points are needed, and for 7 NT, 37.

POSITIVE RESPONSE

This is a general term for a response to an opening forcing bid that shows more than the minimum on which a negative response would be given.

The requirements for a positive response to a forcing-two opening are shown under the Goren and Culbertson systems. The requirements for a positive response to two clubs vary somewhat from one system to another. See *Two-Club Opening*.

PRE-EMPTIVE BID

A pre-emptive bid is one made at an unnecessarily high level in an attempt to crowd the opponents. Its purpose is defensive and obstructive, rather than offensive and constructive.

Pre-emptive openings

An opening bid of three or four in a suit is in nearly all systems a weak shutout bid, based on a long suit with little or no outside strength. In general, a player will overbid by two tricks when vulnerable, by three tricks when not vulnerable, but many players take bigger risks when not vulnerable.

Minor suit three-bids are also weak in standard practice, but some players set a higher standard, requiring a seven-card suit with two of the top three honors. This sometimes enables partner to transfer to 3 NT with fair confidence.

Responses to pre-emptive openings

Any response to a pre-emptive opening, if made in a new suit below the game level, is forcing for one round. In the same way, any advance beyond four hearts or four spades is a slam try.

Pre-emptive overcalls

A double jump overcall, or a higher overcall, is normally based on the sort of hand that would be suitable for an opening pre-emptive bid at the same level. For example:

South	West	North	East
		1♣	3♡

South	West	North	East
		1♠	4◇

A single jump overcall (for example, one spade—three clubs) is pre-emptive in most American systems (see *Weak Jump Overcall*). In Culbertson and most British systems it is a strong call.

Pre-emptive responses

A double jump or higher response in a new suit is pre-emptive. For example:

South	North
1♣	3♠

South	North
1♡	4♠

In general, these pre-emptive responses promise a reasonable expectation of making the contract but deny more than about 6 to 8 points.

Defense to pre-emptive openings

Various conventions have been developed for contesting against an opponent's three-bid (or weak two-bid). See *Fishbein Convention, Lower Minor Convention, Optional Double, Reese Defense,* and *Three No-Trump Take-out.*

PREPARED BID

A player who opens with one of a suit has to have a sound rebid should his partner make a simple response in a new suit. When this consideration influences the choice of opening, the player is said to make a prepared bid.

♠ K Q 10 x   ♡ J x x x x   ◇ x   ♣ A K x

Other things being equal, a five-card suit is bid before a four-card suit. Here, however, a one-heart opening would leave no sound rebid if partner responded two diamonds. Looking ahead, the player should open one spade, for he will then have a convenient rebid over any response from partner.

♠ A J x x   ♡ x x   ◇ K J 10 x   ♣ A J x

The prepared bid is one diamond, for if one spade were opened there would be no sound rebid over two hearts. If the clubs and hearts were interchanged, however, one spade would be in order, for then a response of two hearts could be raised.

♠ A J x x   ♡ x   ◇ K J 10 x   ♣ A Q x x

As on most 4-4-4-1 hands, the prepared bid is the suit below the singleton, in this case, one diamond.

See also *Short Club*.

PROBABILITIES OF DISTRIBUTION

A declarer who has to develop a long suit can judge the likely distribution of the defenders' cards by reference to a table of mathematical frequencies. For example, if declarer has A K Q x x opposite x x x then, in the absence of any further information, the chance of a three-two break is about 68 per cent.

In most hands, of course, other indications are available. One defender may be known to be long or short in another suit, and that will affect the odds. Apart from such indication, the probabilities are as follows:

Two cards will be divided 1-1 fifty-two times in a hundred, 2-0 forty-eight times.

Three cards will be divided 2-1 seventy-eight times, 3-0 twenty-two times.

Four cards will be divided 3-1 fifty times, 2-2 forty times, 4-0 ten times.

Five cards will be divided 3-2 sixty-eight times, 4-1 twenty-eight times, 5-0 four times.

Six cards will be divided 4-2 forty-eight times, 3-3 thirty-six times 5-1 fifteen times, 6-0 once.

Seven cards will be divided 4-3 sixty-two times, 5-2 thirty-one times, 6-1 seven times, 7-0 less than 0.5 times.

As the play of the hand advances, the more even divisions become, in general, more likely. This applies also as an individual suit is played. For example, with A K x x x opposite x x, the chances of a 3-3 break are initially 36%, but when both opponents have followed to two rounds, the chance that the remaining cards will be 1-1 is (at least) 43%. When a *significant* card remains outstanding, such as the queen when declarer has A K J x x opposite x x, the chance is over 50% that the last two cards, the queen and another, will be divided.

PROGRESSIVE SQUEEZE

This is an ending in which the same opponent is subjected to two squeezes in succession. The squeeze wins two tricks for declarer and there must be threats against the same opponent in three suits. In the majority of cases there is an extended threat in the hand opposite the squeeze card.

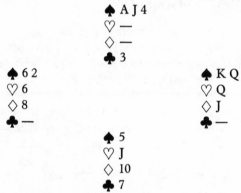

Playing at no trump South leads the seven of clubs. East cannot let go a spade without giving dummy the remaining tricks. And if East discards a diamond or a heart he is squeezed again when that suit is led by South to the next trick.

When there is no extended threat, as in the spade suit above, there must be two two-card threats in different hands and there must also be a one-card threat on the left of the opponent to be squeezed. The minimum compass is five cards.

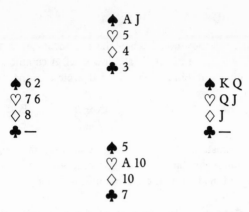

When the seven of clubs is led East is squeezed in three suits. Whichever suit he lets go, he will be squeezed again a trick or two later. Although he has only three clear winners South makes all five tricks.

It was stated above that where there is no extended threat there must be, among other features, a one-card threat on the left of the opponent to be squeezed. If the one-card threat is wrongly positioned—on the right of the opponent to be squeezed—correct discarding will prevent the squeeze from becoming progressive.

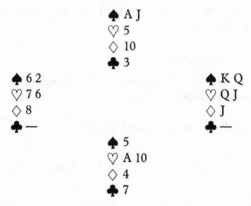

The position is the same as in the preceding diagram, except that South's ten of diamonds has been exchanged for North's four of diamonds.

On the lead of the seven of clubs East must discard a heart to avoid being squeezed a second time. In so doing he follows a principle of discarding, which is to let go the suit that is controlled on his left.

119

PROTECTIVE BID

A protective situation arises when the opponents have opened the bidding and have allowed it to die at a low level. A common example is where an opening suit bid of one is passed around to the fourth-hand player:

South	West	North	East
1♡	Pass	Pass	?

In these circumstances a player may be justified in re-opening the bidding on a moderate hand in the expectation that his partner holds fair values. A bid made in that expectation is called a protective bid, or a "balancing" bid.

Simple overcall by fourth-hand player

In standard practice a simple overcall is the weakest protective bid the fourth-hand player can make. The following would be about a minimum for a protective bid of one spade:

♠ K J 9 x   ♡ x x   ◇ A x x   ♣ x x x x

Some systems carry the protection theory further, requiring fourth hand to re-open with even less high-card strength. These are systems that favor trap passes by second hand.

1 NT by fourth-hand player

A protective 1 NT can be weak, about 11 to 13 points, even when the strong no trump is normally played.

Take-out double by fourth-hand player

The requirements for a take-out double are also relaxed. The following would be a minimum take-out double of one heart in standard practice:

♠ Q x x x   ♡ x x   ◇ K J x   ♣ A x x x

Protective bid on the second round

In match-point pairs, especially, good players will re-open the bidding on the second round on quite moderate values when it is apparent that both opponents are limited.

South	West	North	East
1◇	Pass	1♡	Pass
2◇	Pass	Pass	?

East holds:

♠ K J x　　♡ K 10 x x　　◇ x x　　♣ A 10 x x

For East to re-open with a protective double (which partner might well pass for penalties) would be hazardous but not unknown.

PSEUDO-SQUEEZE

When a declarer leads out a long suit in the hope that an opponent will throw a wrong card, that is a pseudo-squeeze.

An ending that has the form of a genuine squeeze but can nevertheless be defended is more accurately called an imperfect squeeze.

PSYCHIC BID

In the widest sense, any bid that deliberately misrepresents a player's holding may be called a psychic bid. The term is generally applied, however, to an opening bid or overcall that either pretends to non-existent values or names a suit that is not the true one.

The usual occasion for such a bluff is when it seems likely that opponents have the balance of strength and, left to themselves, will reach a game or slam. Thus, the psychist is usually more active when partner has passed and the vulnerability is favorable. Most psychists like to have an "escape" suit, to which they propose to retreat if they are doubled in their psychic suit. The more intrepid, however, do not regard an escape suit as an essential qualification.

There was a considerable vogue for psychic bids in the early days of contract, but the general improvement in bidding has made such tactics less profitable. Modern psychists, in the tournament field at any rate, conduct the battle with three-card suits, lead-inhibiting bids, and other tactical strokes. They go for gentle deflection rather than flagrant deception.

The special provisions for sub-minimum openings that are made by some modern American systems come into a different category (see *Controlled Psychics*).

QUANTITATIVE FOUR NO-TRUMP

A player who has agreed to play a 4 NT convention, such as Blackwood, will sometimes wish to use the 4 NT call in a natural and non-conventional sense. 4 NT is generally regarded as a natural, quantitative call in any of the following circumstances:

(a) When no suit has been mentioned by either partner.

South	North
1 NT	4 NT (not conventional)

(b) When no trump suit has been agreed upon, either directly or by inference, and 4 NT can be interpreted as a natural raise of partner's no-trump call.

South	North
1♠	2♡
2 NT	4 NT (not conventional)

Neither hearts nor spades are agreed by inference, so the 4 NT call is natural.

There are some situations where it may be that the partnership is still searching for a fit, as in an auction of this kind:

South	North
1♠	2♡
3♣	3◇
4♣	4 NT

Many Blackwood bidders would treat 4 NT in this sequence as conventional, but the modern tendency is to regard 4 NT as natural except when a trump suit has been clearly agreed.

A precipitous jump to 4 NT will itself confirm the trump suit. For example:

South	North
1♠	2♡
4 NT	

Here the 4 NT bid is conventional, confirming hearts by inference, for only strong heart support would account for this big jump by a player who had opened with a non-forcing bid.

REBID BY OPENER

Under this heading we consider the opener's first rebid after a suit opening at the one-level and a simple response in a new suit.

Limited bids promising no extra strength

The following rebids show a hand that is in the minimum range of high-card points:

(a) A simple rebid of opener's suit:

South	North
1♦	1♠
2♦	

(b) A rebid of 1 NT showing, in standard practice, a hand in the 13-to-16-point range:

South	North
1♣	1♡
1 NT	

(c) A single raise of partner's suit:

South	North
1♣	1♠
2♠	

Changes of suit that may cover a wide range of strength

A simple change of suit on the second round is not forcing.

South	North
1♦	1♡
1♠	

South's hand may vary from a minimum of 13 points to a hand just short of the 20 to 21 points required for a jump-shift.

A change of suit at the two-level does not necessarily guarantee extra strength when the new suit is lower in rank than the first:

South	North
1♦	1♠
2♣	

When a new suit is bid at the range of three, or a higher-ranking suit is bid at the two-level, the opener promises extra strength. For example:

South	North
1♠	2♢
3♣	

South	North
1♢	1♠
2♡	

These sequences are examined under *Reverse Bid*.

Invitational bids just short of game

(a) A jump rebid of opener's suit after a response at the one-level:

South	North
1♡	1♠
3♡	

This is strong but not forcing.

(b) A jump rebid over a response at the two-level:

South	North
1♡	2♣
3♡	

This is forcing in standard practice.

(c) A jump raise of responder's suit:

South	North
1♣	1♡
3♡	

Strong, but not forcing. Responder may pass on a bare minimum.

(d) A rebid of 2 NT:

South	North
1♢	1♠
2 NT	

This jump shows about 19 to 20 points.

South	North
1♠	2♣
2 NT	

After a response at the range of two, the 2 NT rebid is usually in the 15-to-17-point range.

Game, bids

(a) A jump to game in the opener's suit is a value call, and is thus stronger in playing tricks than a jump rebid.

South	North
1♡	1♠
4♡	

The rebid suggests about 8 or 9 playing tricks, in addition to good honor strength. In systems where strong two-bids are available as well as a forcing two-clubs, the game rebid always implies a good fit for the responder's suit.

(b) A jump raise to game is equally a value call, stronger than a raise to three.

South	North
1♣	1♡
4♡	

The following hand would qualify for such treatment:

♠ x   ♡ A Q 10 x   ♢ K Q x   ♣ A Q J x x

(c) A jump to 3 NT over a response at the range of one shows about 21 points. After a response at the two-level, the jump to 3 NT can be made with a little less:

South	North
1♠	2♣
3 NT	

Here the rebid suggests about 18 to 20 points.

125

Game-forcing rebids

A change of suit combined with a jump on the second round is game-forcing.

South	North
1♢	1♡
2♠	

See *Jump-Shift*.

RECTIFYING THE COUNT

In most cases a squeeze can best be executed when the declarer is able to win all the remaining tricks but one. The maneuver known as rectifying the count is an attempt to bring about that situation.

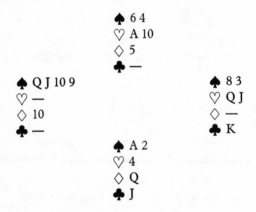

Defending at no trump, West lead the queen of spades. South must hold up his ace, in order to rectify the count.

There are five cards left and declarer has only three natural tricks. If he wins the spade lead the timing will not be right for a squeeze against East: when the squeeze card, the queen of diamonds, is led East will have a spade to throw and will not be embarrassed.

After ducking the queen of spades, declarer can win three of the last four tricks. The timing is right. Declarer wins the next trick, either a spade or a diamond, and plays off his other winner to squeeze East.

This stratagem of ducking an early trick is very common in squeeze play. Whenever there is a prospect of a squeeze, declarer counts the number of cards remaining and tries to bring about the situation in which he can win with top cards all the tricks but one.

See also *Submarine Squeeze*.

REESE CONVENTION

Like the *Maltais Responses to One No-Trump*, this is a way of finding a fit, or establishing a guard, after an opponent has bid two of a suit over partner's 1 NT. The bidding goes:

South	West	North	East
1 NT	2◇	2 NT	Pass
3♣			

North will sometimes bid 2 NT in this sequence without a self-sufficient guard in diamonds. In *Develop Your Bidding Judgment*, Terence Reese proposed that South's rebid of three clubs should have Staymanic implications. At his next turn North may bid 3 NT with a suitable holding in diamonds, or three diamonds with a half-stop like Q x, or three of a major suit on a holding that was too weak to show on the previous round.

The convention is included in the *Little Major*.

REESE DEFENSE

Since the publication of *Blueprint for Bidding*, Acol players have adopted the defense to three bids there recommended. A double of three clubs or three diamonds is primarily for take-out; over three hearts or three spades, 3 NT is for take-out, double is for penalties; in the protective position (when the opening bid has been followed by two passes), double is always for take-out.

Alternative systems of defense are *Fishbein Convention, Lower Minor Convention, Optional Double*, and *Three No-Trump Take-out*.

RELAY-BID

The relay method is used in some systems played by European teams. In certain sequences the responder does not try to give a picture of his own hand but makes a series of relay-bids at the lowest level so that he can learn more about his partner's hand.

An example of a relay-bid at the one-level is found in the Roman system, where one heart in response to one diamond does not show hearts but asks the opener to describe his hand further.

RESCUE-BID

Rescue-bids are usually made by a player whose partner has been doubled in an overcall. For example:

South	West	North	East
1♡	2♣	Double	2♠

East's two spades, if bid on weakness because he was afraid to leave his partner in two clubs doubled, is a rescue.

For two conventions that attempt to put these rescue operations on a more scientific basis see *S.O.S. Redouble* and *Kock-Werner Redouble*.

RESPONSES TO OPENING BIDS OF ONE IN A SUIT

At the one-level

For a response at the one-level (for example, one club—one spade) the minimum strength on normal hands is about 6 points. It can be less when there is a good five- or six-card major suit. There is no precise upper limit to a one-over-one response since any such response in a new suit by a player who has not already passed is forcing for one round. On very strong hands responder will make a jump-shift.

At the two-level

At the two-level a simple response in a new suit promises more strength—upwards of 10 points or slightly less with a good suit.

When an opponent has made an intervening bid a response in a new suit shows more strength (see *Free Bid*).

Choice of suit

In general, when suits are of unequal length, responder shows the longer suit first. An exception occurs when the longer suit would have to be bid at the level of two and the player is not strong enough to bid at that level:

♠ K J x x   ♡ x   ◇ J x x x x   ♣ J x x

Over one heart the response would be one spade, not two diamonds. When the suits are of equal length, a number of factors sway the decision.

As between two five-card suits, the higher ranking is normally preferred.

As between two four-card suits, a suit that can be bid at the level of one is generally preferred to one that would have to be bid at the level of two.

When the suits can both be bid at the same level, the deciding factor, generally, is whether the player proposes to show both suits or only one:

♠ A K x x   ♡ K Q 10 x   ◇ x x   ♣ x x x

Over an opening of one club or one diamond, most players would plan to show both major suits, so their first response would be one spade.

When the hand is weaker, or when it is not intended to show both suits, it is usual to respond with the lower ranking suit:

♠ K J x x   ♡ A J x x   ◇ x x   ♣ x x x

Now the response to one club or one diamond would be one heart, rather than one spade. That has the advantage of giving partner an easy opportunity of showing spades himself.

When the choice lies between two four-card suits at the level of two, once again it is usual to prefer the suit of lower rank. This is especially so when one suit is hearts:

♠ x x   ♡ A J x x   ◇ 10 x x   ♣ A Q x x

Over one spade, two clubs would be preferred to two hearts.

Other responses to a suit bid of one are described under *Double Raise of Suit Opening, Jump-Shift, No-Trump Responses to Suit Opening* and *Pre-emptive Bid*.

RESPONSIVE DOUBLE

This is a conventional call that can be used in certain circumstances by the partner of a player who has made a take-out double. It was first publicized by Dr. F. Fielding-Reid.

When a take-out double has been made and the next player raises the opening call, the fourth-hand player is often faced with an awkward decision:

South	West	North	East
1♦	Double	2♦	?

East holds:

♠ Q 10 x x   ♡ K x x x   ♦ x x   ♣ A x x

There is no certainty that West holds four cards in each major, and if East now calls a suit he may choose the wrong one. Playing the responsive double, East can double two diamonds. Instead of being a penalty double, as in normal practice, that will throw the ball back into partner's court, asking him to name a contract.

Using a double in this sense means that a player can no longer double for penalties in these situations. Supporters of the convention hold that the double is more useful to extract a call from partner.

Whether responsive doubles should be played at the three-level is a matter for partnership agreement. One arrangement is to play responsive doubles up to three of a minor suit and to treat a double of any higher contract as a penalty double.

The convention can also be used when third hand, after a take-out double, bids a new suit at a low level, as in this sequence:

South	West	North	East
1♣	Double	1♠	?

It is possible, but less common, to treat a double by East as responsive.

RESTRICTED CHOICE

A defender's card in certain situations provides the declarer with a negative inference of a special kind. Compare these two combinations:

(1)   A 10 6 2   (2)   A 9 6 2
      K Q 5   K Q 5

In example (1) declarer plays off king, queen, and five. West follows suit, and only low cards have appeared. No special inference can be drawn concerning the position of the jack, and the odds slightly favor a play for the drop.

In example (2) East plays the jack (or ten) on the second round, and again West plays low on the third round. Now a new consideration arises. If East had held J 10 x originally he might have played the jack on the second round or he might have played the ten. The fact that he chose one or the other affords a negative inference that this was his only choice. With J x he *must* play the jack; with J 10 x he *might* have played the ten. His jack is thus more likely to have been played from J x, and declarer should finesse the nine on the third round.

This is called the "Principle of Restricted Choice." Almost all players apply the principle unconsciously in this familiar situation:

A J 10 x x

x x x x

Say that declarer finesses the ten on the first round and loses to the queen. On the next round West plays low. Now there is one card outstanding, the king. It might be thought that East was as likely to hold that card as West, but a player who knows the validity of the principle of restricted choice would play for the finesse. The fact that East has played the queen, when from K Q he might equally have played the king, affords a presumption that he does not hold K Q. It is more likely that his choice was restricted than that he exercised a choice in a particular way.*

REVERSE BID

A player is said to reverse when he first calls the lower ranking of two suits and follows, at the range of two or higher, with a bid of the higher ranking.

South	North
1♣	1♠
2♦	

South	North
1♡	1 NT
2♠	

South	North
1♦	2♣
2♠	

In each of these auctions South's second call is a reverse and North

* For a full account of this difficult subject, see chapter III of *Master Play* (*The Expert Game*) by Terence Reese.

would have to go to the three-level to show preference for South's first-named suit. It follows that South should hold better than a minimum hand. The first suit should be longer and the hand good enough to play at the three-level.

If the distribution is particularly good, say, six-five, then the honor strength need be little more than minimum. A less powerful distribution, such as five-four, requires about 18 points or four honor-tricks. But with a good fit in the responder's suit a reverse bid may be made on a little less strength.

Whether a reverse bid is forcing or not depends, for most players, on whether the opposite hand has shown good values. For example:

South	North
1◇	1 NT
2♠	

Two spades is non-forcing because North's hand is severely limited.

South	North
1♡	2♣
2♠	

After North's two-level response two spades is forcing for at least one round.

A player who bids a second suit at the range of three, as in the sequence one spade—two hearts—three diamonds, is said to show "reversing values," though his second bid is not literally a reverse.

Reverse by the responder

The responder, too, can reverse the bidding as in the following sequence:

South	North
1♡	2◇
2♡	2♠

A responder's reverse is forcing for one-round and generally forcing to game in effect.

REVERSE SIGNALS

The idea of reversing normal signaling methods was put forward by the Austrian expert, Carl Schneider. He questions the merit of the traditional method whereby a high card encourages and a low one discourages.

The main contention is that it is better to encourage with a low card because a high card cannot always be spared.

Q 10 8 2

A 6   K J 9 3

7 5 4

When West leads the ace, East, playing the normal convention, cannot afford the nine as an encouraging card. He must play the three and hope that partner will understand. Playing reverse signals, the three from East would be encouraging. It is also claimed that, when a player wishes to discourage, the play of a high card can convey a more definite message. The following situation is one that often causes difficulty in defense:

6 3

K Q 10 7   9 8 4

A J 5 2

West leads the king against no trump. East plays the four and declarer will usually drop the five as a deceptive measure. Now West cannot be sure of the true position—his partner may be trying to encourage from A 4 2 or J 4 2, not being able to spare an honor, or the four may be his lowest card.

Playing reverse signals, East will drop the nine to discourage a continuation. That will make the situation immediately clear.

Most exponents of reverse signals do not extend the method to such occasions as when a player echoes with four small cards to give his partner a count of a suit. In these positions normal signals are used. Thus, reverse signals are employed only to encourage or discourage a lead.

Theoretically, the method has an over-all advantage, but it has not, as yet, become widely popular.

RIPSTRA

To compete against an opponent's 1 NT opening, J. G. Ripstra of Wichita, Kansas, uses an overcall of two clubs to show a complete or partial three-suiter with short diamonds, and an overcall of two diamonds to show a three-suiter with short clubs. The strength is much affected by vulnerability and the range of the opponent's no-trump.

Players using Ripstra have more chances to land safely than players using *Landy* or *Astro*. Opportunities for the convention are less frequent, however, as there must be preparedness for three suits, including both majors.

ROMAN BLACKWOOD

This variation of *Blackwood* assists the partnership to identify the aces held, especially when the 4 NT bidder holds one ace and his partner two. In the original form of the convention, the responses to 4 NT are:

Five clubs	no ace or three aces
Five diamonds	one ace or four aces
Five hearts	two aces of the same color or rank
Five spades	one of the "odd" combinations (hearts and clubs or diamonds and spades).

The response of five hearts is not always definitive, and many players extend the schedule, using five hearts for two aces of the same color, five spades for two of the same rank, and 5 NT for the two odd combinations. The letters CRO (color, rank, odd) serve as mnemonic. A slight disadvantage of this method is that when the response is 5 NT there is no room for enquiry about kings.

ROMAN GERBER

By applying the *Roman Blackwood* principle to *Gerber* and *Four-Club Blackwood*, and making the maximum use of bidding space, a partnership can go far toward identifying exact holdings in aces, kings and queens.

Four clubs asks for aces. A response of four diamonds shows three aces or none, four hearts shows four or one, and four spades shows two. The next cheapest bid (e.g., four spades after a response of four hearts) initiates enquiry for kings, and enquiry for queens may follow. When the second bid is a range higher (e.g., 4 NT after a response of four hearts) the request is for clarification of the previous response. A responder who has shown, say, one ace, bids the suit in which it is held. If he has shown three aces, he bids the missing suit. If he has shown two aces, he advances one, two or three steps, following the schedule described in *Roman Blackwood.*

ROMAN JUMP OVERCALL

Jump overcalls in the *Roman System* show two-suited hands. The suits are always the suit named and the next higher suit, excluding the suit bid by the opponent. Thus three diamonds over an opponent's one heart would show diamonds and spades.

ROMAN LEADS

See *Rusinow Lead.*

ROMAN TWO DIAMONDS

This opening bid in the *Roman System* shows a strong three-suiter with an average of 17-20 points and 4-4-4-1 or 5-4-4-0 distribution. With a weak hand partner responds in his cheapest four-card suit (even if he has another, longer suit). If this is the opener's short suit he bids the suit immediately above. When responder sees game prospects he bids 2 NT over two diamonds. The opener then names his *short* suit.

It is a weak point in standard systems that an opening bid of one is sometimes passed out when there is an exceptionally good fit in another suit. For this reason many players have incorporated the Roman two diamond bid into their system.

ROMAN SYSTEM

This system is played by the Italian pair, Avarelli and Belladonna. It is essentially a system of distributional bidding.

Balanced hands

Moderate hands of 12 to 16 points are opened one club. Stronger hands of 17 to 20 points are opened one no-trump, and very strong hands, in the 21-25 point range, are again opened one club.

Single-suited hands

Opening bids of one diamond, one heart, and one spade are forcing and normally show a suit of four cards or more. (When holding five clubs, the opener may sometimes have to bid a three-card diamond suit.) A response in the next suit (or one no-trump over one spade) is negative, fewer than 9 points.

Two-suited hands

The shorter suit is bid first. A sequence such as one diamond—one heart—1 NT means that opener has five hearts. There is special treatment for two-suiters that include clubs. The sequence one club—one diamond—1 NT shows both minor suits. Opening bids of two hearts or two spades show at least five of the major and four clubs.

Three-suited hands

Three-suiters in the 12 to 16 range are opened two clubs, and in the 17 to 20 range, two diamonds. For the system of responses, see *Roman Two Diamonds*.

Powerful hands

These are opened with one club, which is thus a three-way bid. This class of hand is expressed by a jump on the next round or by the bid of a minor suit over a negative response.

Defensive bidding

Responses to take-out doubles are made in a short suit (unless third hand has intervened). An overcall of 2 NT shows a strong two-suiter. Responder bids the lower unbid minor. With both unbid suits, the overcaller then bids 3 NT. Overcalls in the opponent's suit are natural.

For other features of the Roman System, see adjoining titles.

ROTH-STONE SYSTEM

This bidding system was developed by Alvin Roth and Tobias Stone. The following are the most important respects in which Roth-Stone differs from standard practice:

Opening bids in first or second position are never "shaded." They are either controlled psychics or else they are completely sound.

In third or fourth position, opening bids may be "shaded" for tactical reasons, as under normal bidding methods, but they are never psychic.

Four-card majors are not opened in first or second position; a three-card minor suit may be opened instead. A rebid of a major shows a six-card suit. Lacking a six-card suit, opener's rebid may be a three-card minor and the responder must allow for this possibility.

Free Bids. Standard requirements for free bids in competitive situations are dealt with under *Free Bid*, *Free Raise* and *Free Rebid*. Roth-Stone lays great emphasis on the need for extra values in all these situations. In general, it may be taken that a free bid of any sort shows a stronger hand than in standard practice.

Responses to opening bids. A response of 1 NT to a major-suit opening is forcing for one round and shows about 10 points. An immediate single raise of a major is constructive and promises 10 to 12 points.

A simple response in a new suit at the two-level is virtually forcing to game and shows a hand as strong as an opening bid.

Pre-emptive bids of three are somewhat weaker than normal. Weak two-bids and weak jump overcalls are played.

In addition, jump free bids and jump responses by an unpassed hand are weak bids based on a long suit and few points.

1 NT opening is strong, showing 16 to 18 points, but the normal responses are reversed. Thus, a response of two in a suit is forcing for one round but a jump to three of a suit is a weak sign-off.

Overcall in the opponent's minor suit (for example West 1◇— North 2◇) shows that suit and is not forcing. Simple overcalls are normal.

Psychic openings are regulation practice on certain holdings in first or second position when not vulnerable. They are made on hands containing from 3 to 6 points with four or more cards in the suit bid, usually including a high card. The psychic bidder normally passes at his next opportunity.

Where the opening bid is a possible psychic (that is to say, where the opener is first or second hand and is not vulnerable) the following responses have a special meaning:

2 NT response shows 20 to 21 points. A psychic opener may pass, raise to 3 NT or rebid his suit. To show a non-psychic opening, he bids a new suit.

3 NT response shows more than 21 points.

Raise to game in a major is very strong, allowing for the possibility of a psychic opening.

Double raise in a major is also strong. If the opener now calls 3 NT, that discloses a psychic opening and asks responder to call four in the major.

Another feature of the system is the *Negative Double*.

RUFF AND SLUFF

When the declarer is able to ruff a defender's lead in one hand, while discarding a loser from the other, he is said to obtain a ruff and discard, often called "a ruff and a sluff." For example:

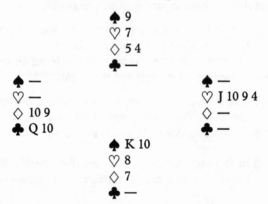

Spades are trump and South exits with a heart. East wins and has to return the suit, giving a ruff and discard. Declarer naturally elects to ruff in dummy and discard the losing diamond from his own hand.

An end position of that kind, where the defender has to concede a ruff and discard, can often be brought about by elimination play. The diagram position resulted from the following simple elimination:

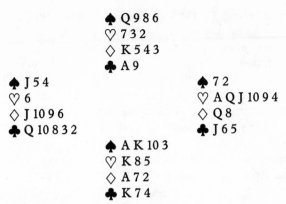

South is playing four spades after East has overcalled in hearts. East wins the first trick with the ace of hearts and returns the queen, which is covered by South and ruffed by West. West leads the jack of diamonds. South wins and draws trumps in two rounds.

Having lost two tricks, declarer still has a loser in each red suit and his only chance to dispose of one is by a ruff and discard. This can be achieved if East started with fewer than three diamonds. Declarer eliminates clubs, ruffing the third round in dummy, and cashes the king of diamonds. Then he puts East in with a heart, as shown earlier.

RUFFING SQUEEZE

A ruffing squeeze is one in which the element of trump enables the declarer to strike down the enemy's guard. It is known also as a trump squeeze.

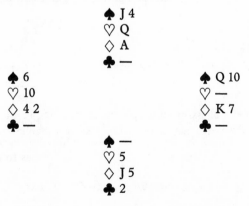

Clubs are trump. On the heart lead East is squeezed. If he discards a spade, South ruffs a spade and North is high. If East throws a diamond North cashes the ace and sets up South's jack.

The situation resembles a criss-cross squeeze, the difference being that a trump takes the place of one of the isolated winning cards. A further difference is that in a ruffing squeeze the lead must be in the hand opposite the trump when the squeeze begins.

Like the criss-cross squeeze, the ruffing squeeze is automatic, since it operates equally well against either opponent.

There are other squeeze endings where the trump element plays a part, but the ending is not by definition a trump squeeze: .

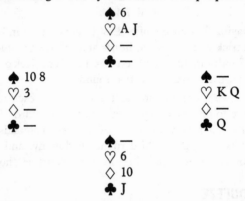

Diamonds are trump and the lead is in dummy. South ruffs the spade and squeezes East in the process.

Here the trump element merely provides an entry. If the lead had been in his own hand South could have brought about an ordinary automatic squeeze by leading his last diamond.

RULE OF ELEVEN

When a player leads fourth best from a long suit the number of that card, when subtracted from 11, will tell how many higher cards are held by the other three hands.

The rule of eleven assists all the players to judge the lie of the cards. It helps the leader's partner in a situation such as the following:

K 10 3

6 led   A Q 8

Defending against no trump West leads the six and dummy plays low. Taking the lead to be fourth best, East applies the rule of eleven. He subtracts 6 from 11 and concludes that there are five cards higher than the six not in the leader's hand. Since all five are visible to him, he can judge that South has no high card. East can play the eight in the assurance that it will hold the trick.

Declarer, also, can apply the rule:

K 8 4

A 10 6 2

West leads the five, dummy plays low, and East's jack is taken by the ace. The rule tells South that East has no other card better than the five. To make three tricks, therefore, he does not try to drop the queen or nine in East's hand. He leads towards dummy and finesses the eight if West does not split his Q 9.

The explanation of the rule is simple. Imagine that the cards are numbered from 2 (the deuce) up to 14 (the ace). By subtracting the number of the card led from 14 we obtain the total number of higher cards in all four hands. Three of those cards are known to be held by the opening leader, so instead of subtracting from 14 we subtract from 11.

RULE OF TWO AND THREE

This is a test whereby a player may judge how much he can risk when making a pre-emptive opening or a defensive overcall. The rule states that, vulnerable, a player can afford to overbid by two tricks, not vulnerable, by three tricks. For example:

♠ x ♡ K Q J 9 x x x ◇ x x ♣ Q J 10

This hand contains about seven playing tricks in a heart contract. Not vulnerable, it would be a fair risk to overbid by three tricks and open four hearts; vulnerable, three hearts would be enough.

The rule is also called The Rule of 500 since, broadly speaking, it is fair to go down 500 to save a game.

RUSINOW LEAD

Some thirty years ago Sydney Rusinow of New York pointed out the advantage of leading the second highest card from a sequence instead of the traditional highest card. Habit was strong, however, and it was not until 1964 that the ACBL sanctioned this type of lead for tournament play. In other countries they are known as Roman Leads.

One obvious gain is that the lead of a king is no longer ambiguous: it means A K not K Q. Also important is that in many cases partner can tell that a lead is from an interior sequence:

Q 6 5

jack led   A 7 4 2

When defending against a suit contract, especially, East may be uncertain whether to take his ace after dummy has played low. Playing Rusinow leads, East knows that his partner has led from K J 10, since with J 10 the ten would be led.

The lead of the second highest is generally carried down to the nine from 10 9. There are, however, some different theories. One is that the queen should be led from Q J or K Q 10 9, that the jack should deny, and the ten guarantee, a higher honor.

Middle cards. Practice varies, also, in respect of the lead from an interior sequence. The Roman players lead the ten from K J 10, the nine from K 10 9. The British style is to lead the higher card from the interior sequence, the jack from K J 10, the ten from K 10 9. In the writer's experience, this method works well.

Partner's suit. When leading partner's suit, it is usual to depart from the convention and lead the highest card. This is because the lead is often made from an unsupported honor like J x, and it would be impractical for the jack to promise the queen.

Later in the play. Rusinow leads are normally made only on the first trick. There is no reason why they should not be used throughout the play, however. An advantage appears in this sort of situation:

K 9 x

queen led   A 10 x x

At some point in the play West, perhaps as a desperation measure, leads an unsupported queen through dummy's K x x. When East holds the ace over the king at least he knows that declarer holds the jack.

SAFETY PLAY

A perfect safety play is one that is safe against any distribution of the opposing cards. A simple example:

AQ963

K 10 7 2

By playing the ace or queen first, declarer makes sure of all the tricks, for if either opponent turns up with J x x x he will be open to a marked finesse.

The term is also freely used of many plays that are not completely safe but offer the best chance of making the required number of tricks in a suit.

764

AQ8532

If South needs all six tricks he must finesse the queen, playing East for K x. If he can afford to lose one trick, the safety play is to lay down the ace and then lead up to the queen. That is a precaution against a singleton king in West's hand, for if the queen is finessed and loses to the bare king South will have to lose a second trick.

The following safety play is less obvious:

K943

AJ75

Here there is a safety play to avoid losing two tricks against any four-one division. South plays the ace and continues with a low card towards the K 9 4. If West shows void, South goes up with the king. If West follows, then South simply covers whatever card is played.

In the wider field of strategy the element of safety enters into most forms of play. The following hand is an example of safety in the development of a suit and in the protection of master cards:

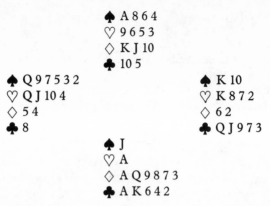

```
                        ♠ A 8 6 4
                        ♡ 9 6 5 3
                        ◇ K J 10
                        ♣ 10 5
        ♠ Q 9 7 5 3 2                    ♠ K 10
        ♡ Q J 10 4                       ♡ K 8 7 2
        ◇ 5 4                            ◇ 6 2
        ♣ 8                              ♣ Q J 9 7 3
                        ♠ J
                        ♡ A
                        ◇ A Q 9 8 7 3
                        ♣ A K 6 4 2
```

Playing six diamonds, South takes the first trick with the ace of hearts. Clearly he has to develop his clubs and, while it is unlikely that it will make any difference, good technique demands that he cross to dummy with the ace of spades for the first lead of clubs. If by any chance East were void of clubs, that would prevent the ruff of a master card.

As it is, the ace of clubs wins, and now comes the critical play: South must lead a low club from his hand. East wins and returns a trump, but there are still two trumps in dummy with which to ruff two club losers.

If South plays off the ace and king of clubs, West will ruff the second round and lead a trump. South will be left with three club losers and only two trumps on the table.

SAN FRANCISCO CONVENTION

This is a 4 NT convention in which kings, as well as aces, are taken into account by the responder. Counting each ace as 3 points and each king as 1 point, the partner of the 4 NT bidder responds according to the following scale:

With less than 3 points	— 5♣
With 3 points	— 5◇
With 4 points	— 5♡
With 5 points	— 5♠
With 6 points	— 5 NT

And so on.

The San Francisco Convention has an advantage over Blackwood on certain occasions. For example:

	South		North
	1♡		4♡
	4 NT (San Francisco)		5♠

South can now place North with precisely one ace and two kings, for there is no other way of making up five points.

On other occasions, the 4 NT bidder may be able to tell how many aces and kings his partner holds by reference to the honors in his own hand.

SCHENKEN SYSTEM

Systems using an artificial one club opening for strong hands have long been a feature of the bridge scene. This one has the authority of Howard Schenken of New York City. It is sometimes known as the Big Club.

One club opening. Shows 17 points in high cards or distribution. Any response but one diamond shows at least 9 points (or two aces) and is game-forcing. After a negative response of one diamond, a jump rebid in a suit is forcing for one round. A rebid of 1 NT shows 19 or 20 points, 2 NT shows 21 or 22. Stayman is used after no-trump rebids.

When there has been a positive response to one club, a jump rebid shows a solid suit, and a double jump rebid a long suit with one high card missing.

If the opening one club is overcalled by an opponent, a double shows the values for a positive response. At the three level or over, the double is for penalties.

Opening one spade, one heart, or one diamond. These are limited to a maximum of 16 points. The bidding is developed naturally.

Two diamond opening. This is forcing to game except for the sequence two diamonds—two hearts (no ace)—2 NT, which shows 23 to 25 points.

Partner's first response to two diamonds shows aces. With no ace he responds two hearts. With the ace of hearts he bids 2 NT, and with any other ace he bids the suit in which it is held. A jump response shows the ace of that suit and a lower ace.

After any response to two diamonds, a relay (the cheapest bid) by the opener asks for kings, and a further relay asks for queens. Responses are on the same pattern as for aces. When two aces (or kings or queens)

145

have been shown, a bid of diamonds asks for the second ace to be named.

Apart from these specialized rebids, any continuation is natural.

In case of intervention, a double is not for penalties but indicates the ace of the suit called. Any other bid has the same sense as though there had been no intervention.

Two clubs and *1 NT* are natural openings. *Two hearts* and *two spades* are *Weak Two-Bids*. *Three clubs* denotes a solid suit with little strength outside. Other *three-bids* are pre-emptive. Opening bids of *2 NT* and *3 NT* are strong, but are based on a long solid suit.

SCHENKEN TWO DIAMONDS

This distinctive feature of the *Schenken System* (see above) has been adopted by players of other systems. For other uses of two diamonds, see *Mexican Two Diamonds, Roman Two Diamonds,* and *Stayman Two-Diamond Opening.*

SCISSORS COUP

This is a form of avoidance play in which declarer snips the defenders' only line of communication at an early stage. Culbertson called it the "Coup Without a Name." It has since been named the "Scissors Coup."

Often the object of the coup is to prevent a defender from ruffing:

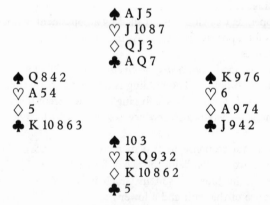

```
              ♠ A J 5
              ♡ J 10 8 7
              ◇ Q J 3
              ♣ A Q 7
  ♠ Q 8 4 2              ♠ K 9 7 6
  ♡ A 5 4                ♡ 6
  ◇ 5                    ◇ A 9 7 4
  ♣ K 10 8 6 3           ♣ J 9 4 2
              ♠ 10 3
              ♡ K Q 9 3 2
              ◇ K 10 8 6 2
              ♣ 5
```

South is playing three hearts and the defense begins with a diamond lead, followed by a diamond ruff. West then leads a small spade.

The defense now threatens to make a second ruff. If South continues

146

in the normal way, going up with the ace of spades and leading a trump, West will win with the ace of trumps and put his partner in with a spade for another diamond ruff.

As the cards lie, declarer avoids that outcome by winning West's spade at trick three, then laying down the ace of clubs, followed by the queen of clubs, on which he discards his losing spade. That has the effect of severing the defenders' only line of communication.

If East were able to cover the queen of clubs with the king, declarer would have to abandon the coup. He would ruff and lead a trump, hoping that the defense would not be able to achieve a second ruff.

SHARPLES FOUR CLUBS

This invention of the brothers R. and J. Sharples of London is aimed at reaching delicate slams in a minor suit after a 1 NT opening. South opens a strong no-trump and North holds:

♠ K Q 3 2   ♡ A J 9   ◇ K 4   ♣ Q 10 8 3

North responds with a Stayman two clubs and on the next round, over a rebid of two diamonds or two hearts, jumps to four clubs. The message is: "I have precisely four clubs and that may be the spot for a slam. If you cannot co-operate in any way, sign off in 4 NT. If you have a fit for clubs, either raise or cue-bid in another suit."

A jump to four diamonds, after a similar sequence, has the same sense of proposing a slam in diamonds.

A bid of three clubs or three diamonds may be made on a longer suit and offers partner a choice of game contracts. It is only the jump to four clubs or four diamonds that asks for the 4-4 fit.

SHORT CLUB

A short club (or "prepared" club) is an opening bid on a short club suit such as often has to be made in the approach-forcing systems. For example:

♠ A Q x x   ♡ Q 10 x   ◇ J x x   ♣ A J x

This hand is not strong enough for a standard 1 NT opening and the objection to one spade is that the player would have no sound rebid over a response in a new suit at the two-level. (That objection would not arise if partner had already passed.)

The solution is to open with a bid in the three-card club suit. A short minor suit may also be opened when the four-card major is unbiddable. For example:

♠ 10 x x x   ♡ A K x   ◇ Q x x   ♣ A K x

Most players would open one club, rather than one spade or 1 NT.

In systems that require five cards for a major-suit opening, three-card minor suits are opened more frequently. When the hand contains only two clubs, one diamond is preferred.

SHORT-SUIT GAME TRIES

When the opener makes a try for game after a sequence like one spade—two spades, he will normally bid a secondary suit like K 10 x x, where he looks for cards that will fill in. Short-suit trial bids rest on the theory that it is more helpful to name a short suit, either a void or singleton, where filling cards are *not* wanted. Opposite such a trial bid, a holding such as x x x or x x x x is a "good" fit, whereas K J x x would suggest wasted values.

It is possible to extend the principle to a later round:

South	North
1♠	2♠
3♣	3♡

In the *Kaplan-Sheinwold* system, where these bids were first developed, both three clubs and three hearts would be game tries on a short suit. Most players take the view, however, that the theoretical gain in accuracy is balanced by the amount of information given to the opponents.

SIGNALING

For a player who is not on lead, the standard way of signaling interest in a suit is to play an unnecessarily high card, usually a seven or higher. This applies generally, both when the player is following suit and when he is discarding.

A more positive message can be conveyed by playing high-low with any two cards (see *Echo*).

Conversely, to discard or follow suit with the lowest available card, or to fail to echo with two cards, suggests lack of enthusiasm for that suit.

See also *Echo*, *Reverse-Signals*, *Suit-Preference Signal* and *Trump Echo*.

SIGN-OFF BID

A sign-off is a bid that proclaims weakness and suggests, in most cases, that the bidding should proceed no further. It usually takes the form of a minimum bid in the agreed suit or in the player's own suit. For example:

South	North
1♣	1♠
2♣	2 NT
3♣	

South's three clubs is a sign-off, denying the ability to call 3 NT or support spades.

In British systems, especially Acol, there are more sign-off bids than in standard American methods. Thus, in the following sequences, the minimum rebid of the player's own suit over 2 NT is a sign-off in Acol:

South	North
1♡	1♠
2 NT	3♠

South	North
1♠	2♣
2 NT	3♣

Equally, since 2 NT in response to an opening bid is non-forcing in Acol, one heart—2 NT—three hearts is a minimum rebid that can be passed.

A negative response is often loosely described as a sign-off.

SKINNER PSYCHIC CONTROL

In some modern systems low responses like 1 NT or the single raise of a minor suit are forcing for one round. Col. Richmond Skinner of Wilmington, Delaware, has pointed out that such responses lend themselves to psychic control (see *Controlled Psychics*). A responder who has the values for a raise of one spade to four spades, for example,

149

interposes 1 NT on the first round, so that if partner is psychic he can pass. When this principle is followed, an immediate raise to game in a major, or a response of 2 NT or 3 NT means that the responder expects to make this contract even opposite a psychic opening.

SMOTHER PLAY

This term describes an ending in which life is denied to an apparently certain trump winner held by a defender.

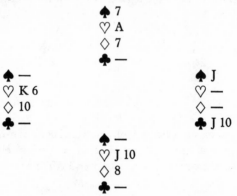

South is playing a heart contract and the lead is in dummy. West, holding K x, with the bare ace on the table, appears to have a sure trump trick, but this vanishes when declarer leads the seven of spades from dummy and discards his losing diamond. East has to lead a club. South plays the ten of trumps and West's king can only gasp and die.

The ending arose from the following hand:

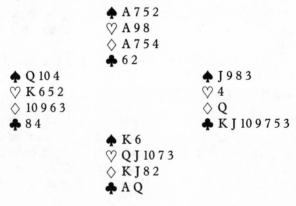

South is playing six hearts after East has made a pre-emptive opening of three clubs.

South captures the club lead and runs the queen of hearts. When this holds, he follows with a low heart, finessing the nine. On the lead of a low diamond from dummy East plays the queen, and on the next round of diamonds East throws a club.

Declarer now knows that he has a diamond loser and his only chance is to bring off a smother play. He takes three rounds of spades, ruffing the third, cashes a second club, and crosses to dummy with the ace of diamonds. The position then is as shown in the first diagram.

S.O.S. REDOUBLE

This is a redouble that is intended, not as a sign of confidence that the player will make his contract, but as a request to partner to rescue into another suit.

There are certain situations where it follows from the logic of the bidding that a redouble must be intended as a distress signal. This is a common occasion for an S.O.S. redouble:

South	West	North	East
1♣	Double	Pass	Pass
Redouble			

South has opened a moderate club suit and knows that the clubs are stacked against him. If he were satisfied with the contract he would not redouble.

The following sequence is different because of the positional factor:

South	West	North	East
1♣	Pass	Pass	Double
Redouble			

This redouble is strength-showing. The distinguishing factor is that the double has not been passed by partner, as it had in the previous example. If, in the present sequence, South did not want to risk being left in one club doubled, he would have to bid another suit himself.

There are other situations where, given good partnership understanding, it will be apparent that a redouble is S.O.S. rather than natural. For example:

151

South	West	North	East
1♡	1♠	Double	Pass
Pass	1 NT	Pass	Pass
Double	Redouble		

It is clear from the bidding that West is on the run and that he wants partner to bid one of the minor suits.

For an extended use of the S.O.S. redouble, see *Kock-Werner Redouble*.

SQUEEZE

When an opponent is forced to throw away winning cards, or cards that protect winners, he is said to be squeezed. The basis of squeeze play is that two hands, say those of declarer and dummy, may contain between them more vital cards than one opponent can protect. When one opponent needs to keep winners or guards in more than one suit, pressure of space may compel him to relinquish his hold on one suit or the other.

The technique of squeeze play is complicated, and even in the simplest three-card ending (which is the minimum compass for a squeeze) certain basic elements have to be present, such as threat cards, entries, a squeeze card and correct timing. All are present in this example of a simple squeeze:

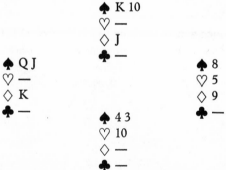

Playing no trump, South lays down the ten of hearts and West is squeezed; he must either unguard spades or throw away the winning diamond.

The threat cards are the ten of spades and the jack of diamonds. Only West can guard against those threats. The spades are described as a two-card threat. The diamond is a one-card threat.

The entry is North's king of spades. There must always be an entry to the hand that is not on lead when the squeeze begins; that is to say, the hand opposite the squeeze card.

The squeeze card is South's ten of hearts, the card which compels West to make the fatal discard.

Correct timing is present in that the position is "tight." West has no idle card that he can throw when the squeeze begins. It is a usual, but not invariable, condition for a squeeze that the declarer should be able to win by top cards all the remaining tricks but one.

The various aspects of squeeze play are described under the following headings:

Automatic Squeeze, Criss-cross Squeeze, Double Squeeze, Entry Squeeze, Guard Squeeze, Jettison Squeeze, Overtaking Squeeze, Progressive Squeeze, Pseudo-squeeze, Rectifying the Count, Ruffing Squeeze, Squeeze without the Count, Submarine Squeeze, Suicide Squeeze, Threat, and *Vienna Coup.*

SQUEEZE WITHOUT THE COUNT

In most squeezes no trick is lost after the squeeze card has been played. That is not an invariable condition, however: a defender who has controlling cards in two suits sometimes wins a trick after the squeeze has begun. That is known as a squeeze without the count.

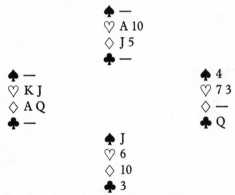

Playing no trump South has only two top winners. He cannot rectify the count for a squeeze, but if he plays his squeeze card now, the jack of spades, he forces West to let go a diamond. Dummy throws a heart, a diamond is conceded, and dummy's jack of diamonds wins the last trick.

153

The various forms of end play often overlap. In the next example declarer exerts pressure in space—the hallmark of a squeeze—on the way to executing a throw-in.

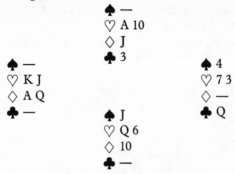

Again the jack of spades compels West to relinquish a diamond winner. Then he is thrown in to lead away from the king of hearts.

STANDARD AMERICAN

The bidding style of most North American players, corresponding to the *Goren System*. Except where otherwise stated, the methods described in this book are Standard American.

STAYMAN AFTER INTERVENTION

See *Maltais Responses to One No-Trump* and *Reese Convention*.

STAYMAN AFTER NO-TRUMP REBID, RESPONSE, OVERCALL

There are various situations where Stayman enquiry takes place on the second round of bidding, and not immediately over a no-trump opening. For example, in systems where two clubs (or one club) is artificial, a sequence like two clubs—two diamonds—2 NT—three clubs is Stayman. In the *Schenken System* one club—1 NT—two clubs is Stayman.

It is possible, though not standard, to treat two clubs as Stayman after a natural rebid of 1 NT:

South	North
1♣	1◇
1 NT	2♣

Players who often open three-card minor suits, and who use the 1 NT rebid to show a precise point-count, may treat two clubs in this sequence as Stayman.

Stayman after a no-trump overcall

Stayman can be used by the defending side in response to a 1 NT overcall.

South	West	North	East
1♣	1 NT	Pass	2♣

Again it is practicable, though not standard, to treat two clubs as Stayman. If the opening bid had been in a major suit, two clubs would ask only for the unbid major.

Stayman by the opening bidder

An opening bidder who has concealed a major suit may use Stayman in this sequence:

South	North
1 NT	2 NT
3♣	

It is possible, though not standard, for three clubs to be Stayman.

STAYMAN CONVENTION

This is the name generally used for the convention whereby two clubs in response to 1 NT is treated as an artificial bid, asking the opener to show a four-card major. Goren stipulates that the major suit should be as good as Q x x x.

South	North
1 NT	2♣

North might hold :

♠ Q J x x   ♡ K J x x   ◇ A x x x   ♣ x

If the conventional two-club bid elicits a major suit from partner, North intends to raise to game in that suit. Otherwise he can revert to no trump.

In its simplest form the opener, if he does not possess a four-card major, always rebids two diamonds; there the convention ends. Goren plays it this way.

There is no general agreement as to which suit the opener should bid if he has both majors. The authorities mostly recommend that spades be bid.

It is, however, accepted that the convention should be abandoned after an intervening double:

South	West	North	East
Pass	1 NT	Double	2♣

Now the two-club call is natural.

The convention has been developed and extended in many directions. The main points of Stayman's own version are set out below.

The Stayman Convention proper

If, after the response to two clubs, the two-club bidder makes a minimum call in a major suit, that promises some values and is forcing for one round:

South	North
1 NT	2♣
2◇	2♡

South	North
1 NT	2♣
2♡	2♠

In each case North's second bid is forcing for one round. A minimum holding would be about 8 points and a five-card suit.

If the responder's second bid is three clubs, that is a sign-off. But three diamonds is another conventional bid and is game-forcing:

South	North
1 NT	2♣
2♡	3◇

South	North
1 NT	2♣
2◇	3◇

Over three diamonds the opener must describe his hand further. He may, for example, show a three-card major.

The sequence 1 NT—two clubs—2 NT is rare. It shows a maximum no trump with probably a strong minor suit.

The convention is also freely used over higher no-trump bids, such as an opening 2 NT or 3 NT.

For additional Stayman variations, see *Double-Barreled Stayman, Maltais Responses to One No-Trump, Murray Two Diamonds, Reese*

Convention, Sharples Four Clubs, and *Stayman after No-Trump Rebid, Response, or Overcall.*

STAYMAN TWO-DIAMOND OPENING

In the system devised by Samuel Stayman of New York two spades and two hearts are *Weak Two-Bids,* while two diamonds and two clubs express different types of strong hand.

Two diamonds takes the place of the normal strong artificial opening of two clubs. The negative response is two hearts.

Two clubs shows a strong hand, usually just short of a game force. Responder always bids two diamonds and opener rebids to show one of four types of hands:

1. *Rebid in a major suit,* at any level, indicates a one-suited hand.

2. *Three club rebid* shows a three-suited hand with a five-card major suit and a void in a minor suit.

3. *Three diamond rebid* indicates a minor two-suiter.

4. *Two no-trump rebid* shows a balanced hand just short of a normal 2 NT opening—19 or 20 points.

By providing additional machinery for expressing powerful hands, this convention repairs one of the failings of *Standard American,* in which opening suit-bids of one carry too great a load. A similar system for two-bids was devised independently by the Scottish player, Albert Benjamin, and is known in Britain as the *Benjamin Convention.*

SUBMARINE SQUEEZE

This describes a maneuver whereby the declarer establishes the right timing for a squeeze.

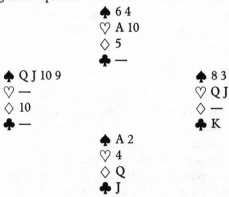

It was noted under *Rectifying the Count*, that when West leads the queen of spades declarer must play low from hand. Two tricks later he will be able to squeeze East.

Now suppose that, in the diagram position, South has the lead. To create the situation in which he can win all the tricks but one, he plays a low spade from hand. This makes the timing right for a squeeze two tricks later.

SUICIDE SQUEEZE

When a defender plays a card that squeezes his partner, that is known as a suicide squeeze.

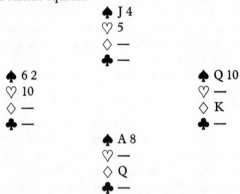

West is on lead, defending against no trump. If he leads his winning heart he squeezes his partner, who has to discard in front of South. West can save the position by not playing off his winner.

It is a common stratagem at no trump for the declarer to give a defender the chance to run off winners in his long suit. That will often have the effect of subjecting the other defender to pressure that he cannot withstand.

SUIT-PREFERENCE SIGNAL

This signaling method differs from others in that its message relates to suits other than the one in which the signal is made. Its invention is credited to the American player, Hy Lavinthal, but it is often called the McKenney Convention, having being publicized by W. E. McKenney. It has been universally adopted by good players.

The convention proposes that the play of an unnecessarily high card should be treated as a request for partner to lead the higher ranking of the other two side suits, provided it be clear from the general situation that partner's choice of lead must lie between those two other suits. The most clear-cut occasion is when a player leads a card for his partner to ruff. He can indicate by his choice of card which of the two remaining side suits should be returned.

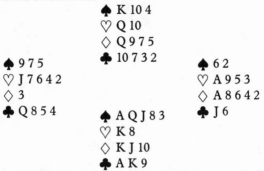

♠ K 10 4
♡ Q 10
♢ Q 9 7 5
♣ 10 7 3 2

♠ 9 7 5
♡ J 7 6 4 2
♢ 3
♣ Q 8 5 4

♠ 6 2
♡ A 9 5 3
♢ A 8 6 4 2
♣ J 6

♠ A Q J 8 3
♡ K 8
♢ K J 10
♣ A K 9

Against four spades, West leads the three of diamonds and East wins. Reading his partner for a single diamond, East returns the eight for him to ruff. This indicates that his quick re-entry is in hearts, and West gets another ruff to set the contract.

That is a suit-preference signal in its simplest form. Its use can be extended to many other situations where there is a choice of cards to play, provided that the signal cannot be confused with a normal encouraging or discouraging signal. For example:

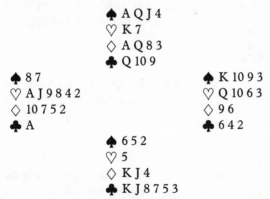

♠ A Q J 4
♡ K 7
♢ A Q 8 3
♣ Q 10 9

♠ 8 7
♡ A J 9 8 4 2
♢ 10 7 5 2
♣ A

♠ K 10 9 3
♡ Q 10 6 3
♢ 9 6
♣ 6 4 2

♠ 6 5 2
♡ 5
♢ K J 4
♣ K J 8 7 5 3

South is playing five clubs after hearts have been bid by West and supported by East. West starts with the ace of hearts and East drops the queen to show that he wants a spade switch, not a diamond.

The convention can be used in no trump as well, for in practice a defender can almost always narrow the choice of suits to two.

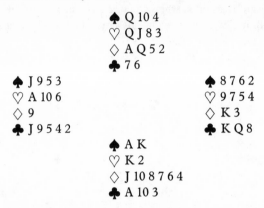

```
              ♠ Q 10 4
              ♡ Q J 8 3
              ◇ A Q 5 2
              ♣ 7 6
♠ J 9 5 3                    ♠ 8 7 6 2
♡ A 10 6                     ♡ 9 7 5 4
◇ 9                          ◇ K 3
♣ J 9 5 4 2                  ♣ K Q 8
              ♠ A K
              ♡ K 2
              ◇ J 10 8 7 6 4
              ♣ A 10 3
```

South is playing 3 NT after showing diamonds in the bidding. West leads the four of clubs and East takes the first two tricks with the queen and king. On the second round West plays the two, a natural card showing his five-card suit.

When East plays the third round of clubs West has a choice of cards to play. Playing suit-preference signals he will drop the five, showing that his entry is in hearts, not spades. Diamonds, being declarer's suit, can be left out of the reckoning.

Holding the ace of spades instead of the ace of hearts, West would play the jack of clubs at trick three. Holding no entry and not wishing to express interest in either suit, he would play a middle card, the nine.

SUPER BLACKWOOD

This is an extension of the Blackwood Convention for situations where 4 NT would be interpreted as a natural bid. For example:

South	North
1♠	2♣
3 NT	4 NT

Many players would treat 4 NT in this sequence as a natural call, a quantitative raise of no trump, not Blackwood.

Suppose, however, that North did want to inquire about aces. Playing Super Blackwood, he would do so by calling four of the lowest-ranking unbid suit:

South	North
1♠	2♣
3 NT	4◇

Now four diamonds, a call of the lowest-ranking unbid suit, asks for aces. The responder shows aces on the step system:

To show no aces or four aces, he calls the next higher-ranking suit. (In the above example, South would show no aces or four aces by calling four hearts.)

To show one ace, he calls the next suit but one, and so on. (In the above example four spades would show one ace, 4 NT two aces and five clubs three aces.)

Asking for kings

After the ace-showing response, the Super Blackwood bidder may call 5 NT as in ordinary Blackwood, to ask for kings. 5 NT guarantees that the partnership holds all four aces.

SWISS CONVENTION

After an opening one heart or one spade, the comparatively idle responses of four clubs and four diamonds are used to express "good" raises to four of the major. The convention is particularly useful for players who use limit jump raises and consequently need to distinguish between a distributional raise to game and a raise based on a fair quota of high cards. For such players, the Swiss response corresponds to the standard forcing raise.

There is no general agreement about the distinction between four clubs and four diamonds. In the Acol system four diamonds promises three aces or two aces and the king of trumps. Alternatively, four diamonds may stress the trump holding, and four clubs the high cards outside the trump suit. A third possibility is for four clubs to promise a singleton, four diamonds more high cards but no singleton.

TAKE-OUT DOUBLE

This is a double of an opponent's low contract, not for penalties but as an invitation to partner to take out into his best suit.

South opens one diamond and West holds:

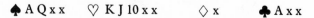

♠ A Q x x   ♡ K J 10 x x   ◇ x   ♣ A x x

To show that he has good values and wants to know where his partner's strength lies, West makes a take-out or "informatory" double.

Distinguishing a take-out from a penalty double

The following definition holds good for all situations except a few that arise in match-point play:

If partner has already made a bid of any kind, then a double is a penalty double made with the expectation of defeating the contract.

If partner has not made a bid, a double of one or two in a suit is for a take-out if made at the first opportunity of doubling.

The logic of the situation is that if partner has already shown by a bid where his strength lies, there is no point in doubling for a take-out.

The following examples illustrate the two types of double:

South	West	North	East
1♡	Pass	2◇	Double

A take-out double, because partner has not made a bid.

South	West	North	East
1♡	1♠	2◇	Double

A penalty double, because partner has already shown his suit.

South	West	North	East
1♠	Double	2♡	Double

West's double is for a take-out, East's for penalties.

South	West	North	East
1♡	2♣	Pass	Pass
Double			

Partner has not made a bid and South's double is at the first opportunity of doubling. It is therefore a take-out double.

South	West	North	East
1♡	Double	Pass	Pass
2◇	Double		

The first double is for a take-out, the second for penalties. It is true that partner has not bid, but his pass to one heart doubled was a penalty pass, showing strength in hearts and thus equivalent to a bid.

South	West	North	East
1◇	Pass	1♠	Pass
2◇	Double		

West's double is for penalties, for he had an opportunity to double for a take-out on the previous round.

South	West	North	East
1◇	Pass	2◇	Pass
Pass	Double		

In tournament play this would be regarded as a take-out double. Technically, it is an exception to one of the rules set out above, for West is not doubling at his first opportunity; but North-South are clearly limited in strength and West is in a protective position.

South	West	North	East
1◇	Pass	1 NT	Pass
2◇	Double		

This is the kind of indeterminate situation that East would resolve according to the nature of his hand. West might have a penalty double or he might wish to compete, knowing that both opponents were limited. It is a situation that cannot be judged away from the table.

A double of 1 NT is primarily a penalty double. The meaning of the double of an opponent's three-opening is a matter of partnership agreement. See *Pre-emptive Bid*.

Requirements for a take-out double

A take-out double promises at least the strength of an opening bid. It also suggests support for the unbid suits. The following would be about a minimum for a take-out double of one club at equal vulnerability:

♠ A Q x x   ♡ K 10 x x   ◇ K x x x   ♣ x

In systems that use a weak jump overcall a player may make a take-out double with a strong one-suited hand. Playing the weak jump over-call, a defender would double one diamond on this hand, where other players would prefer two hearts.

♠ A x   ♡ A K J 10 x x   ◇ x x   ♣ Q J x

The requirements for a take-out double can be shaded when the opening bid has been followed by two passes (see *Protective Bid*). A double at the range of two naturally calls for greater strength.

Responses to a take-out double

Suppose that the bidding has begun in this fashion:

South	West	North	East
1◇	Double	Pass	?

1. With zero to about 7 to 8 points East makes a minimum response in a suit. A player who has a choice of suits in which to respond normally gives preference to a major suit.

2. With a stopper in the enemy suit and some values, about 7 to 9 points, East bids 1 NT. Some players bid 1 NT on a fair balanced hand even when they have no stopper.

3. With great strength in diamonds, East may pass (see *Penalty Pass*).

4. With a useful hand of 9 points or more East jumps either in a suit or no trump. These jump responses are limit-bids and are not forcing, even for one round, though they are invitational. The following would be a minimum for a jump response of two spades:

♠ Q J x x x   ♡ Q x x   ◇ x x x   ♣ A x

5. The strongest call that East can make is a bid in the enemy suit. This is forcing to game in most systems.

Had North, in the above auction, made any bid over the double, East would have been absolved from the necessity of responding on a weak hand.

Should North redouble, East can pass with a bad hand, but should show any useful feature. It would be right to mention a five-card major, for example, even on a very weak hand.

Action against opponent's take-out double

After a take-out double by second hand, accepted practice for the third-hand player is as follows:

1. With a fair balanced hand, about 10 points upwards, he re-doubles.

2. With a moderate hand but support for partner's suit, he raises to the limit. A double raise in this sequence is pre-emptive and not forcing.

3. With a fair to moderate hand he may make a normal response, such as 1 NT or a suit-bid at minimum level. This suit-bid is not forcing.

4. With a long suit and few high cards, he may jump in the suit. A sequence such as one diamond—double—two spades is not forcing.

5. With the values for a sound double raise, he first redoubles and later supports. But see also *Two No-Trump over a Double*.

6. With a weak hand, or a moderate hand containing no feature worth showing, he passes.

See also *Responsive Double*.

TEMPO

This term relates to the element of time in card play, with special reference to the use of opportunities to make an attacking lead.

Thus, a player who makes a neutral move when positive action is required is said to "lose a tempo."

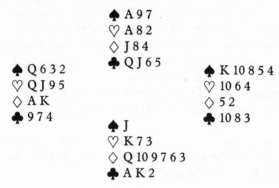

South is playing in five diamonds, which can be beaten only by repeated heart leads. If West opened a top trump, with the idea of having a look at dummy, he would lose a vital tempo. Even if West switched immediately to hearts, declarer would be able to drive out the remaining trumps before the defense could establish a heart trick. Declarer would then have time to discard a heart on dummy's clubs.

TEXAS CONVENTION

This is a bidding device based on the transfer principle. Its object is to place the contract in the strong hand when there has been an opening bid of 1 NT or 2 NT.

When the responder has a long major suit he bids the next lower-ranking suit at the four-level. The opening bidder then transfers back to the real suit, the next higher-ranking. Thus, the no-trump bidder becomes declarer and the player with the long trump suit becomes dummy.

South	*North*
1 NT	4♢
4♡	Pass

South	North
2 NT	4♡
4♠	Pass

The object of transferring the declaration in this manner is to conceal the strong hand from the defenders, and to avoid an opening lead through the no-trump hand. For example, North holds:

♠ K   ♡ A 10 x x x x x   ◇ x x x   ♣ x x

South opens 1 NT and North decides that he is prepared to play for game in hearts. Because of the weakness in the minor suits it may be better that the lead go up to South. North, therefore, bids four diamonds and South transfers to four hearts. Had North, with a different type of hand, been content to be declarer, he could have forced with three hearts and followed with four hearts.

Over an opening 2 NT, North would use the convention in the same way. He would respond four diamonds and raise four hearts to six hearts.

The convention is not normally used for minor suits, although it is theoretically possible to use four spades as a request for clubs, and five clubs as a request for diamonds.

South African Texas

A variation originating from South Africa has both a psychological and a technical advantage. Responder bids four clubs to ask for four hearts and four diamonds to ask for four spades. There is then less likelihood of the no-trump opener forgetting the convention, as he may do when he hears the familiar response of four hearts. The technical advantage of this method is that the no-trump opener, if well suited to the strain proposed by the Texas response, has room in which to interject a cue-bid:

South	North
1 NT	4◇
4♡	

North's four diamonds asks the opener to bid four spades, and South's four hearts is a slam suggestion at a safe level.

Texas opening-bid

Opening bids of four clubs and four diamonds can be used on the

Texas principle, asking responder to bid four hearts or four spades. Three advantages arise:

1. When the convention is used, the declaration is placed in the hand more likely to contain tenaces.

2. The opener can use the convention to distinguish between weak and strong pre-empts. On

♠ K Q J 10 x x x   ♡ x   ◇ Q 10 x x   ♣ x

he opens four spades. With a stronger hand such as

♠ x   ♡ A Q 10 x x x x x   ◇ A x   ♣ x x

he opens four clubs.

3. After the stronger openings, four diamonds and four clubs, responder has room in which to make a slam suggestion (by bidding the intermediate suit) without going beyond game.

For an extension of the transfer principle to a lower level of bidding, see *Jacoby Transfer Bids*.

THIRD HAND OPENING

A player who opens the bidding third hand (after two passes) will choose his bid on somewhat different principles from a player in any other position. The differences arise from the following considerations:

1. Opener does not have to rebid

When a player opens the bidding in first or second hand he has to have a sound rebid over any suit response by his partner. That affects the choice of opening on this type of hand:

♠ K Q 10 8   ♡ Q 3   ◇ Q 9 6 2   ♣ K J 4

The textbook opening first or second hand is one diamond, for if the opening is one spade there is no sound rebid over a response of two hearts. Opening third hand, a player is not obliged to rebid. He can, therefore, disregard the principle of preparedness and open one spade. That is certainly a better bid than one diamond, for the suit is better and the bid has some pre-emptive value in that an opponent cannot overcall so easily.

2. Opportunity for sub-minimum opening

Third hand is best placed at the table for a semi-psychic opening:

♠ K Q 10 7 4   ♡ 5 3   ◇ A 8 4 2   ♣ 6 3

This would not be a sound opening first or second hand, but in third position a sub-minimum bid of one spade is a reasonable risk, especially not vulnerable. The opener can pass any response by his partner, so is unlikely to run into a big penalty. By opening, he indicates a good lead to his partner and makes it more difficult for the opponents to reach their best contract.

3. Wider range of pre-emptive bids

Third hand is tactically well placed to extend the accepted range of pre-emptive bids. If he is very weak, and his partner has passed, he knows that the enemy have a game and quite likely a slam. So, a desperate overbid may show a profit.

Equally, third hand can open with a game bid on hands normally too strong for such a call.

♠ 6   ♡ K Q J 9 8 6 5   ◇ A Q 10 2   ♣ 8

First or second hand, the book opening would be one heart. An opening bid of four hearts could well result in a missed slam. However, after partner has passed, the prospect of slam is much less, and the advantage of pre-empting before opponents can get together is greater.

For a method of protecting weak openings, see *Drury Convention*. For other responses to third-hand openings, see *Jump-shift* and *Passed Hand*.

THREAT (OR MENACE)

To execute a squeeze, a player must hold at least two cards that threaten the same opponent. Observe this position.

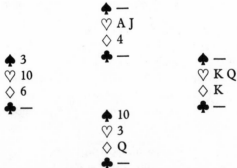

South leads the ten of spades, throwing dummy's four of diamonds. East is squeezed because he is threatened by two cards, the queen of diamonds and the jack of hearts. The queen of diamonds is a one-card threat, the ace and jack of hearts a two-card threat.

Because of entry requirements, there must always be a two-card threat in the hand opposite the squeeze card. (In the above example, the squeeze card is South's ten of spades.) In some variations, however, the two-card threat need not contain a card of top rank.

Technical terms for various kinds of threats are:

Double threat, when the two-card threat exercises pressure against both opponents.

Extended threat, necessary for most forms of progressive squeeze. This occurs when the two-card threat is accompanied by one or more low cards which will be winners if the opponent releases his guard. In the example above A J x in hearts would be an extended threat.

Isolating the threat, a process whereby a threat originally controlled by both opponents is isolated so it can be defended by one opponent only. For example, with A K x x opposite x x of a plain suit, declarer ruffs out the third round. Then the last card will be a threat that only one opponent can defend.

Recessed threat, an extended menace headed by two winners, such as A K x opposite a singleton. A recessed threat, providing extra space in the opposite hand, may offset a disadvantageous arrangement of the other threats.

Split, or divided threat, when the key cards of a two-card menace are in opposite hands, as in the combination Q x opposite A x, with the opponent's K J in between.

Threat-transfer, when control of a threat is transferred from one defender to the other. For example:

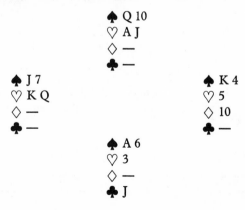

Playing no trump with the lead in dummy, declarer leads the queen of spades, forcing East to cover with the king. This transfers the spade threat to West, who is squeezed when the jack of clubs is led to the next trick.

THREE NO-TRUMP OPENING

An opening bid of 3 NT in standard practice shows a balanced hand with about 25 to 27 points. Over this, four clubs is Stayman and any other response is constructive.

Many players, however, especially those who use an artificial two clubs for strong hands, play the "gambling 3 NT." They make the bid on hands that contain a solid minor suit (minimum A K Q J x x or A K Q x x x x) and not more than a queen outside. Played in this fashion, the 3 NT opening has the pre-emptive value of a minor suit opening at the four-level and at the same time does not exclude a final contract of 3 NT.

Responding to the gambling 3 NT

Knowing the character of the opening bid, responder must make the decision whether to play in 3 NT or in the minor suit, and at what level.

The examples that follow are from *Blueprint for Bidding* by Reese and Dormer.

(1) ♠ Q 10 x   ♡ A x x x   ◇ Q J 9 x   ♣ x x

Responder should take his chance on making 3 NT.

(2) ♠ A x x x   ♡ x   ◇ 10 x x   ♣ K Q x x x

Responder can jump to five diamonds (knowing that diamonds must be the suit). Without the ace of spades the jump would still be right as a defensive measure.

(3) ♠ A K x x x   ♡ J x   ◇ x x x   ♣ x x x

Now responder takes out into four clubs. If partner's suit is diamonds he will transfer.

(4) ♠ A K x x   ♡ J 10 x x   ◇ K Q   ♣ x x x

With this hand, prospects of making 3 NT are good. If opponents double, it is not necessary to redouble, for the opening bidder will stand his ground.

THREE NO-TRUMP TAKE-OUT

By partnership arrangement, a call of 3 NT over an opponent's three opening can be used as a request for a take-out. The bid is then equivalent to a strong take-out double. It does not show a guard in the enemy suit. In the same way, 2 NT can be used as a request for a take-out over opponents' weak two-bids.

The partner of the 3 NT bidder will normally take out into his best suit. He will pass only when he holds a guard in the enemy suit and judges 3 NT to be the best contract.

As a take-out request, 3 NT is wasteful of space over a double of three clubs or three diamonds. For that reason, most Acol players have switched to the *Reese Defense*. See also *Fishbein Convention, Lower Minor Convention,* and *Optional Double.*

THROW-IN

In the classification of end plays the term throw-in is used especially for the situation in which declarer throws the lead to an opponent who has to play into a tenace combination. This is the simplest form:

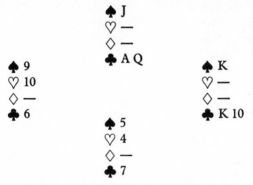

Having reason to place East with both black kings, South exits with a spade and East has to lead into the club tenace.

At no trump a defender is often thrown in with his own long suit. This is a typical example: (*See hand on next page.*)

South is playing 3 NT after West has made an overcall of one spade.

West leads the king of spades and South captures the second round, East discarding a club. It would be a mistake to hold up for two rounds, for then declarer would have no card of exit with which to throw the lead.

To have any chance of nine tricks South must find East with the diamond king, so he crosses to dummy with the king of hearts and runs the queen of diamonds. He continues with the jack of diamonds and then a third diamond to the ace, West throwing a club.

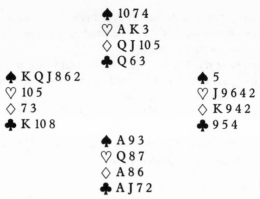

♠ 10 7 4
♡ A K 3
◇ Q J 10 5
♣ Q 6 3

♠ K Q J 8 6 2
♡ 10 5
◇ 7 3
♣ K 10 8

♠ 5
♡ J 9 6 4 2
◇ K 9 4 2
♣ 9 5 4

♠ A 9 3
♡ Q 8 7
◇ A 8 6
♣ A J 7 2

When diamonds fail to split declarer needs two tricks from clubs. If he places West with the king of clubs for his overcall, he can make the contract by a throw-in.

His next move is to take a second and third round of hearts on which West has to make another discard. If West throws a spade, South can place him with exactly three spades and two clubs. He then executes a throw-in by playing a spade, forcing West to lead up to the clubs at trick twelve.

A good defender in West's position would throw two clubs rather than a club and a spade. South would then have to judge whether to finesse in clubs or to play for the drop of the now unguarded king.

TOP OF NOTHING LEAD

When a player leads his highest card from two, three or more worthless cards, he is said to lead "top of nothing." To lead the higher card of a doubleton is standard practice, but there is less uniformity in the lead from three or more small cards.

Lead from three small cards

The older practice is to lead the top card from a holding like 6 4 3 and to follow with the 4. As noted under *Lead against No-Trump*, however, many players now lead the middle card from three and follow with the top card—the system known as MUD (Middle, Up, Down).

Lead from four or more small cards

Against a trump contract the choice of card depends on the circumstances. It is usual to lead a middle card, or the top card, of an unbid suit, but to lead fourth best of partner's suit. If the leader has supported his partner, however, suggesting either length or strength, it may be clearer to lead the top card from four small.

Against no-trump, fourth best is normal. The top card might be led from a sequence like 9 8 7 x x.

TRANSFER BIDS

See *Jacoby Transfer Bids* and *Texas Convention*.

TRIAL BID

A trial bid is one that can be recognized as a try for game, not necessarily indicating strength in the suit named. The usual occasion for the bid is after a single raise in a major:

South	North
1♠	2♠
3◇	

South's three diamonds is a trial bid. It is forcing and does not put forward diamonds as an alternative contract. It is, in all probability, a try for game in spades, though on an exceptional hand South may have slam aspirations.

In judging his action over the trial bid, whether to sign off in three spades or go to game, responder will be influenced by his holding in diamonds. The trial bid will usually be made in a suit wherein opener hopes to find some values opposite. Thus, he will not make the bid on a singleton, though he may on x x x.

Since the bid of a new suit after a single raise is a game try, many players treat a raise to three (one heart—two hearts—three hearts) as pre-emptive. When the opener is not strong, but has a fair suit, he bids three hearts to make it more hazardous for the last player to re-open.

See also *Short Suit Game Tries*.

TRUMP ASKING-BIDS

A convention for locating key cards in the trump suit, trump asking-bids are designed for use in conjunction with Culbertson asking-bids. After a normal asking-bid and response, a bid of 4 NT is a trump asking-bid. Partner responds according to his holding in the trump suit, as follows:

Trump holding (irrespective of length in the trump suit)	Response
No top honor (A K Q)	5 clubs
One of three top honors	5 diamonds
Two of three top honors	5 hearts
All three top honors	5 spades

If, after a response to a trump asking-bid, the 4 NT bidder now calls 5 NT, the other player has to show his trump length:

Trump length	Response
Three trumps or fewer	6 clubs
Four trumps	6 diamonds
Five or six trumps	6 hearts
Seven or more trumps	6 spades

If the response to the normal asking-bid is at the five-level, 5 NT can be used as a trump asking-bid for honor cards but it is not possible to follow up by asking for trump length.

See also *Grand Slam Force*.

TRUMP CONTROL

When declarer can draw the opposing trumps and hold the lead after forcing out the last trump against him, he is said to possess trump control.

There are many tactical moves open to a declarer who is threatened with loss of trump control. One rests on his timing in the trump suit itself.

♠ 8 4
♡ 10 7 3 2
◇ A K
♣ Q J 7 3 2

♠ A K J 10 6
♡ 5
◇ 10 7 4 3
♣ A K 6

Hearts are led against South's four-spade contract and he has to ruff the second round. If he enters dummy with a diamond in order to finesse spades, he may lose control. Say that West wins and plays another heart: South ruffs again, but he has now been shortened twice and if the trumps were originally four-two he will not be able to draw them.

The safe play for ten tricks, after ruffing the second lead, is to lay down the ace and king of trump and then, if the queen does not fall, play clubs. The opponents will make two trump tricks, but that will be all against any normal break.

Another move in the battle for trump control is to refuse to ruff until dummy is void in the suit that is being attacked.

♠ J 7
♡ 7 5 4
◇ K Q 8 6 2
♣ 10 5 4

♠ A K Q 10 6
♡ 10 3
◇ J 10 5
♣ A K 6

Against three spades the defense begins with three rounds of hearts. If South ruffs and draws trumps he will be in trouble if the spades are four-two, for the ace of diamonds will still be out. A possible plan is to ruff the third heart and force out the ace of diamonds while dummy has a trump with which to deal with another heart lead. But the opponents may be able to hold up the ace of diamonds for one round and collect a diamond ruff. That will leave declarer with a losing club.

The safest play is to throw the losing club on the third round of hearts, loser-on-loser play. The contract will then be safe unless the opponents take an immediate diamond ruff. That is not likely, for had there·been a singleton they would probably have led the suit earlier.

TRUMP COUP

Many coups center round the trump suit, but the term trump coup is generally reserved for the following kind of end position:

(See hand on next page.)

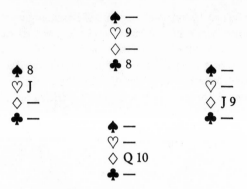

Diamonds are trump and if South is on lead he has to lose a trick. With dummy on lead, however, declarer brings off a trump coup to take both tricks. In effect, he takes a trump finesse against East though dummy has no trump to lead. That is the essence of the trump coup.

It is usually when the trumps break badly that declarer has to try for a trump coup. Thus the above ending results from the following hand:

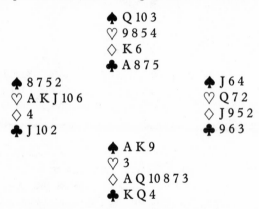

Defending six diamonds, West leads the ace and king of hearts and South ruffs. South lays down the king and ace of trumps and when the 4-1 break is revealed he realizes that his only hope lies in a trump coup against East. To achieve this he must shorten his trumps to the same length as East's. His plan depends on East's having to follow suit while the plain suit winners are cashed.

After the second round of trump, therefore, South crosses to dummy and ruffs another heart. Then he cashes the top tricks in the black suits to reach the ending shown above, with the lead in dummy.

176

It will be noted that West's play of a second heart at trick two helped South to shorten his trumps. An expert defender might have foreseen that possibility and switched to a black suit at trick two. In that event declarer would have to take the precaution, when in dummy with the king of diamonds, to use that entry for a heart ruff.

See also *Grand Coup* and, for some different types of coups in the trump suit, *Coup en Passant*, *Devil's Coup* and *Smother Play*.

TRUMP ECHO

There is a convention dating from auction bridge whereby an echo in the trump suit shows a tripleton, not a doubleton as in other situations. This echo can be employed in a general way to give a partner a count, but most players hold that it is more useful to reserve it for occasions when there is a possibility of obtaining a ruff. Thus, the echo may carry a twofold message to partner.

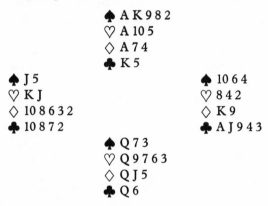

♠ A K 9 8 2
♡ A 10 5
◇ A 7 4
♣ K 5

♠ J 5
♡ K J
◇ 10 8 6 3 2
♣ 10 8 7 2

♠ 10 6 4
♡ 8 4 2
◇ K 9
♣ A J 9 4 3

♠ Q 7 3
♡ Q 9 7 6 3
◇ Q J 5
♣ Q 6

West leads the three of diamonds against four hearts. Dummy plays low, East wins with the king and returns the nine. On these two tricks South plays the jack and the queen, so that West cannot be sure whether East started with two or three diamonds. Capturing the second diamond South leads a small trump to the ace, East starting an echo with the four. West takes the next round of trumps while his partner completes the echo with the two. This shows that East has a third trump, and West leads another diamond to defeat the contract.

If East had held a slightly different hand—three diamonds and A Q x x of clubs—he would not have echoed in trump and West would then have switched to a club after winning with the king of hearts.

TRUMP PROMOTION

A trump promotion occurs when the defenders create extra trump tricks by a tactical maneuver. One common example is the Uppercut, which is described under that title. The other effective method of trump promotion is to lead a plain suit through declarer, who has to ruff in front of the other defender. The extra trick is often created by refusal to overruff, as in the following example:

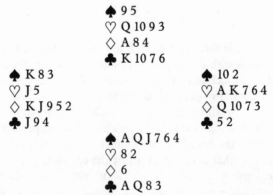

Suppose this is the layout of the trump suit. East is on play and he leads a plain suit of which both South and West are void.

If South ruffs with an honor and West overruffs with the ace, declarer will be able to draw the defenders' trumps as soon as he gets in. If, however, West declines to overruff, he will subsequently win two trump tricks.

There are innumerable variations of that theme. Sometimes the prospect of a trump promotion is less obvious than in the above example, but a defender should be guided by the principle that it is usually wrong to overruff when holding a sure trump winner. For example:

Against four spades West leads the jack of hearts which is covered by the queen and king. East plays ace and another heart and declarer ruffs with the queen of trump.

Though the prospect of a second trump trick is uncertain, it cannot profit West to overruff, so he discards. When partner turns up with the ten West collects two trump tricks.

TRUSCOTT CONVENTION

See *Two No-Trump over a Take-out Double*.

TWO-CLUB OPENING

The tendency of modern bidding is toward a conventional two-club opening in place of the forcing two-bid. Among tournament players in Britain the forcing-two is almost extinct.

Requirements for two-club opening

Since the two-club opening is forcing to game, with one or two exceptions as mentioned below, the first requirement is that the hand should be of game-going strength. Some systems, such as Acol, make the further requirement that five or more honor-tricks should be held, except on hands of no-trump type on which the rebid will be a non-forcing 2 NT.

In systems in which two clubs is the only forcing opening, there are generally no stipulations as to points or honor-tricks. In general, such systems require merely a hand of game-going strength. Stayman, for instance, gives this example of a two-club opening:

♠ A   ♡ A K Q J 7 5 3   ◇ Q 6   ♣ K 9 4

In Acol, that would qualify for a two-heart opening, forcing for one round. Stayman, and most other American systems that use the conventional two-club opening, use weak two-bids in other suits, and therefore open two clubs on this hand.

Responses to two-club opening

The negative response is always two diamonds. For a positive response, the requirements vary from system to system but the popular style is to give a positive response with 8 or more points and a good suit, and to bid 2 NT on a scattered 7 to 10 points with no strong suit.

Some systems, such as Stayman, require specific holdings for a positive response, such as an ace and a king, or a king-queen in one

179

suit and a king in another. The Acol system originally had a list of such requirements but that has now been abandoned. The present method in Acol is to bid a fair major suit when holding one plus honor-tricks, or a minor suit when holding $1\frac{1}{2}$ honor-tricks. 2 NT is called on a balanced 9 points or more.

When two clubs is not game-forcing

In Acol, and systems that use the same style of two-club opening, the following sequence shows a balanced hand of 23 to 24 points and responder can pass on complete weakness:

South	North
2♣	2♢
2 NT	

With a stronger hand the opener can rebid 3 NT.

In some systems the bidding is allowed to die short of game when opener repeats his major suit at minimum level, as in the following sequence:

South	North
2♣	2♢
2♠	2 NT
3♠	

Responder with a worthless hand can pass three spades.

Other two-club conventions

For special ways of using the two-club opening, see *Jacoby Two-Bids* and *Stayman Two-Diamond Opening*.

TWO-CLUB SYSTEMS

Many players now use two clubs as an artificial forcing bid, in place of the forcing two, but in most respects their bidding conforms to standard practice.

In the British *Acol System*, two clubs is game-forcing with one exception and other two bids are forcing for one round. Many British players follow a style called "Utility," in which two clubs is forcing to game and other two bids are of intermediate variety, strong but not forcing. Since more hands are opened with a two-bid than in the approach-forcing systems, opening bids of one do not cover so wide a range and need not be kept open on minimum values. It is a simple way of bidding, well suited to players who have not a close partnership understanding.

TWO-DIAMOND OPENING

Ineffective as a weak two bid, inessential on a strong hand containing diamonds, the two-diamond opening has become the plaything of modern theorists. For different ideas, see *Mexican Two Diamonds, Roman Two Diamonds, Schenken System,* and *Stayman Two-Diamond Opening.*

TWO NO-TRUMP OPENING

In standard practice, 2 NT shows a balanced hand of 22 to 24 points with at least one guard in each suit. Many players prefer the range common in Britain, about 20 to 22. See also *Mexican Two Diamonds.*

Responses to 2 NT

Any response in a suit is forcing. Three clubs is usually played as Stayman, asking for a major suit. In another variation, three clubs asks the opener to call his lowest-ranking four-card suit. Three diamonds then promises a diamond suit but does not necessarily deny a major suit. A rebid of 3 NT means that the opener's only four-card suit is clubs. See also *Flint Convention* and *Texas Convention.*

TWO NO-TRUMP OR THREE ARTIFICIAL RAISE

Many American players have adopted limit raises and no longer play one heart—three hearts and one spade—three spades as forcing. In place of such techniques as the *Delayed Game Raise* and the *Swiss Convention,* some use an immediate response of either 2 NT or 3 NT to denote a traditional game-forcing hand—13 to 15 points with adequate trump support.

When 2 NT is used for this purpose, conventional meanings can be attached to the opener's rebids. It is common for the opener to bid four of his suit as a sign-off and three of his suit on a stronger hand. A bid of a new suit can be employed to show a singleton, void, or any other feature.

TWO NO-TRUMP OVER A TAKE-OUT DOUBLE

After partner's opening one heart or one spade has been doubled for a take-out, 2 NT can be used by the responder to express a fair hand worth a natural raise to three. (There is no need for 2 NT as a natural bid, for with all-round values responder would redouble.) After the 2 NT response the opener must bid the game himself when not minimum. This convention is standard among tournament players in Britain, where it is known as the *Truscott Convention*.

TWO NO-TRUMP OVER ONE NO-TRUMP FORCING

Players who have a narrow range for their opening 1 NT may dispense with a natural raise to 2 NT. (Responder either passes or bids a close game.) In the *Baron System* a response of 2 NT is forcing and requires the opener to show his four-card suits in turn, beginning with the lowest-ranking. This enables the partnership to discover their best fit.

TWO-OPENING

Opening bids of two in a suit are forcing to game in standard practice. See *Forcing Two-Bids*.

Many tournament players use an artificial two-club opening for strong hands. Two hearts and two spades are weak in some systems (see *Weak Two-Bid*) and strong in others.

See also *Jacoby Two-Bids, Schenken System, Stayman Two-Diamond Opening*, and *Two-Club Systems*.

TWO-WAY FINESSE

This is a finesse that can be taken against either opponent. Usually, a queen or jack is the missing card:

A J x x

K 10 9

South can play either opponent for the queen.

At a trump contract a different kind of two-way finesse can arise:

A Q J x

x

Suppose this is a plain suit in which South needs two tricks. He can take a simple finesse against West or a ruffing finesse against East.

UNBLOCKING PLAY

This is the play of an unnecessarily high card, usually with the object of allowing a subsequent trick to be won in the opposite hand. The following are some of the principal occasions for unblocking:

To facilitate the run of a suit

A x

Q J 10 9 x   K x x

x x x

Defending against no trump, West leads the queen and dummy holds up the ace. When West continues with the jack, East must unblock by throwing the king.

Declarer often has to make the same sort of play:

K 10 9 x

x   J x x

A Q 8 x x

Suppose declarer wants to run this suit. In order to guard against a possible 4-0 break in either hand, he starts by laying down a top card from his hand. At the same time he must be careful to unblock with dummy's 9 or 10. Otherwise, he may find himself trapped on the table on the fourth round of the suit.

Unblocking for a finesse

Playing the following combination at no trump, declarer has no outside entries to dummy:

A K 9 8 x

Q x x   x x

J 10 x

Declarer plays the ace from dummy, then comes to his hand for a finesse. Unless declarer has unblocked by throwing jack or ten under the ace, West can block the suit by playing the queen on the second round.

In the next example South observes a standard play but he also needs to unblock:

A Q 8 x x

10 x x x   J

K 9 x

Correct technique is to lead up to the ace, then a small card back to the king; this discovers a finesse if East holds the singleton jack or ten. However, South must lead the nine to the first trick, for otherwise he will not be able to run the suit.

Unblocking to create an entry

Sometimes a player can gain an extra entry by unblocking:

K 6 4 2

J 5   10 9 7

A Q 8 3

Declarer leads the ace and queen, then the eight to dummy's king. By preserving the three he establishes an extra entry to the table.

The next example is of a spectacular unblock by the defense:

A x

J 9 x   K x

Q 10 x x x x

To establish an entry for his partner, East unblocks with the king when dummy plays the ace.

A counter to avoidance play

Unblocking play can be a complete answer to a declarer who tries to establish a suit while keeping the dangerous defender out of the lead (see *Avoidance Play*):

K 8 x x

J 9 x   Q x

A 10 x x

Wishing to keep West out, declarer leads a small card toward dummy. West inserts the nine, so dummy has to put on the king. East then unblocks with the queen.

Unblocking to avoid an end play

There are many elimination and throw-in positions where it is essential for the defenders to unblock:

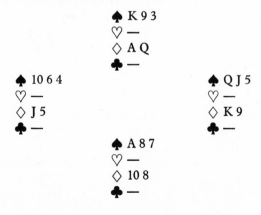

South requires four more tricks at no trump. When the ace and king of spades are led out, East must execute a double unblock so as not to be thrown in on the third round.

In a final example West has to escape a ruff and discard elimination:

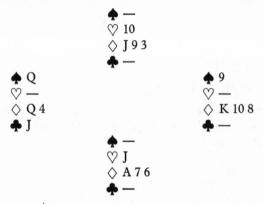

```
                    ♠ —
                    ♡ 10
                    ◇ J 9 3
                    ♣ —
    ♠ Q                         ♠ 9
    ♡ —                         ♡ —
    ◇ Q 4                       ◇ K 10 8
    ♣ J                         ♣ —
                    ♠ —
                    ♡ J
                    ◇ A 7 6
                    ♣ —
```

Playing in hearts, declarer has eliminated the side suits. When South plays the ace of diamonds, West must unblock by throwing the queen. Otherwise he will have to win the next diamond trick (for East cannot afford to overtake) and lead a black card, allowing South to ruff on table and discard his other loser.

UNUSUAL NO-TRUMP

This convention was developed by Alvin Roth, of New York City, and has been widely accepted by good players.

As originally conceived, the essence of the convention was that an unusual bid in no trump, a bid that could hardly be genuine, should be regarded as a take-out double based on length in the minor suits.

Suppose that South holds:

♠ x   ♡ x x   ◇ K Q x x x   ♣ A 10 x x x

These are some of the sequences in which he might introduce an unusual no trump:

South	West	North	East
	1♡	Pass	1 NT
Pass	2♡	Pass	Pass
2 NT			

South	West	North	East
Pass	1♡	Pass	1♠
1 NT			

South	West	North	East
	1♡	Pass	2♠
2 NT			

Good players soon began to extend the use of the unusual no trump to other situations in which they wished to contest the bidding on a distributional hand. Suppose that South, not vulnerable, holds the following hand against vulnerable opponents:

♠ x   ♡ J 9 x x x   ◇ x   ♣ A 10 x x x x

The bidding goes:

South	West	North	East
	1♠	Pass	2◇
2 NT			

Theoretically this bid of 2 NT could be genuine, but it would be wanted in that sense so seldom that a partnership playing the unusual no trump would take it the other way, showing willingness to contest in the unbid suits. The strength of North's own hand would surely tell him whether the 2 NT bid was natural or "unusual."

The unusual no-trump can also be used by a player who has previously made a natural bid:

South	West	North	East
1♡	2♣	2♡	Pass
Pass	2 NT		

West might hold:

♠ x   ♡ K x   ◇ A Q x x   ♣ K Q 10 x x x

West's 2 NT indicates that he can contest in either minor suit.

In a final example a player who has opened the bidding employs the unusual no-trump.

South	West	North	East
1◇	2♠	Pass	4♠
4 NT			

South's 4 NT cannot be natural or Blackwood. It can only mean that he wishes to compete further. If his second suit were clubs he could bid five clubs, so the correct inference is that he has a powerful red two-suiter.

UPPERCUT

This is a descriptive term for a familiar kind of trump promotion. A defender ruffs as high as he can, though he expects to be overruffed, in the hope of promoting his partner's trumps.

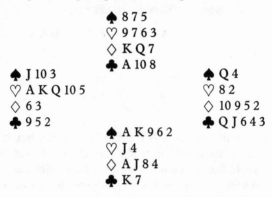

South is playing four spades and West leads out three rounds of hearts. If East ruffs the third round with the queen declarer must lose two trump tricks.

To make sure that his partner will ruff high West can lead a low heart on the third round. East will then realize what is expected of him.

In the following example, it is the dummy that is uppercut:

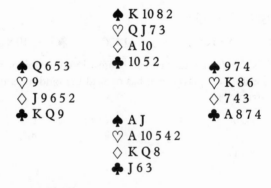

Against four hearts West leads king, queen and another club. East wins and judges that the setting trick can come only from trumps, so he plays the thirteenth club. West uppercuts with the nine of hearts, forcing the jack from dummy; that leaves East with a certain trump trick.

VANDERBILT CLUB

This one-club system was developed by Harold S. Vanderbilt of New York in the early days of contract bridge and has been revised by him to form the basis of the modern Vanderbilt system. Apart from specialized bids, it uses the same principles as the *Schenken System.*

VIENNA COUP

This is an unblocking play that is sometimes necessary before declarer can benefit from a squeeze position. Consider the following diagram:

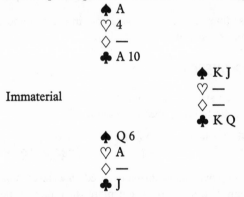

Declarer has all the material for a squeeze against East, who has to guard both spades and clubs. However, if declarer lays down the ace of hearts East will discard a spade and declarer will not benefit because the spades will be blocked.

Declarer must first play off the ace of spades, unblocking that suit. Then, on the heart return, East will be squeezed.

In technical terms, the Vienna Coup consists of the play of the top-ranking card of a suit so that a card of lower rank will be correctly positioned as a one-card threat in an automatic squeeze.

189

VIENNA SYSTEM

Played by the Austrian team in the nineteen thirties, this was the first of the successful artificial systems. Among modern systems, it is closer to Roman than any other.

An opening one club was limited, with one diamond a weakness response, and 1 NT game-forcing. Other suit openings promised five cards. An opening 1 NT served for almost all strong hands. Two clubs was the weakness response to this, and two diamonds then asked for major suits. The *Herbert Convention* was used in many situations.

VOID-SHOWING BID

By agreement, a double jump in a new suit can be used to show a void in the suit named and strong trump support.

(1)	*South*	*North*	(2)	*South*	*North*
	1♣	1♠		1♡	1♠
	4♢			2♣	4♢

In each case four diamonds shows a void in the suit and strong support for partner's last suit.

WEAK JUMP OVERCALL

Most American systems use a jump overcall as a mildly pre-emptive measure when the bidding goes as follows:

South	*West*	*North*	*East*
		1♡	2♠ (or 3♣ or 3♢)

The weak jump overcall is normally based on a six-card or longer suit and a total high-card strength of not more than about 9 points. Some systems, such as Roth-Stone, make the bid on a very weak holding indeed.

The jump overcall is also weak when both opponents have spoken, as in this sequence:

South	*West*	*North*	*East*
1♢	Pass	1♡	2♠ (or 3♣)

In Culbertson and most British systems the jump overcall is strong in all positions. See *Jump Overcall*.

WEAK NO-TRUMP

Many partnerships use a weaker no-trump opening than that of standard systems. The range of strength is usually from 12 to 14 or 13 to 15 points.

In the *Kaplan-Sheinwold* system a weak no-trump is used throughout. Many players use a strong no-trump when vulnerable, a weak no-trump when not vulnerable.

Some partnerships play what is called a "three-quarters no-trump." This means that 1 NT is weak except when the partnership is vulnerable and the opponents are not.

See also *Woodson Two-Way No-Trump.*

WEAK TWO-BID

Most systems that have two clubs as their forcing bid use two spades, two hearts, and in some cases two diamonds, as a weak bid showing a strong six-card suit and a total of about 7 to 11 points. This is a typical two heart opening bid:

♠ x x   ♡ A Q J x x x   ◇ x x   ♣ Q 10 x

Responses to weak two-bids

A single raise of a weak two is generally treated as a further pre-emptive effort, not a constructive bid. Any other response short of game is forcing for one round.

Opener's rebid after a forcing response

After a response of 2 NT, a simple rebid by opener shows that he holds minimum values. He can show a better hand by bidding a new suit, even a short suit. In this event he will give preference to a suit in which a high card is held.

After any other forcing response the players bid naturally.

Defense to weak two-bids

Against opponents' weak two-bids, many players use the same defensive method as against weak three-bids—such conventions as Fishbein, optional double, no-trump take-out, or lower minor. More straight-forwardly, a double can be for a take-out, with 2 NT showing a guard in the enemy suit.

See also *McCabe Adjunct*, a device enabling responder to play in a suit of his own choice at the three level.

WOODSON TWO-WAY NO-TRUMP

An opening 1 NT with extremities so far apart that there is a mountain between them. The bid is made either on 10 to 12 or 16 to 18. A response of two clubs inquires for the range, the opener bidding two diamonds or two hearts (slightly stronger) when in the 10-12 range, and two spades or 2 NT when 16 to 18. A rebid of three clubs by the opener is Stayman. If responder wants to ask about the major suits he bids three diamonds.

An alternative possibility is for the opener always to rebid two diamonds (which may be the limit) when he has the weak no-trump. With the strong hand he can bid two hearts when he has some interest in the major suits, and otherwise two spades or 2 NT, according to the range.

A CATALOGUE OF SELECTED DOVER BOOKS
IN ALL FIELDS OF INTEREST

A CATALOGUE OF SELECTED DOVER BOOKS
IN ALL FIELDS OF INTEREST

AMERICA'S OLD MASTERS, James T. Flexner. Four men emerged unexpectedly from provincial 18th century America to leadership in European art: Benjamin West, J. S. Copley, C. R. Peale, Gilbert Stuart. Brilliant coverage of lives and contributions. Revised, 1967 edition. 69 plates. 365pp. of text.
21806-6 Paperbound $3.00

FIRST FLOWERS OF OUR WILDERNESS: AMERICAN PAINTING, THE COLONIAL PERIOD, James T. Flexner. Painters, and regional painting traditions from earliest Colonial times up to the emergence of Copley, West and Peale Sr., Foster, Gustavus Hesselius, Feke, John Smibert and many anonymous painters in the primitive manner. Engaging presentation, with 162 illustrations. xxii + 368pp.
22180-6 Paperbound $3.50

THE LIGHT OF DISTANT SKIES: AMERICAN PAINTING, 1760-1835, James T. Flexner. The great generation of early American painters goes to Europe to learn and to teach: West, Copley, Gilbert Stuart and others. Allston, Trumbull, Morse; also contemporary American painters—primitives, derivatives, academics—who remained in America. 102 illustrations. xiii + 306pp.
22179-2 Paperbound $3.50

A HISTORY OF THE RISE AND PROGRESS OF THE ARTS OF DESIGN IN THE UNITED STATES, William Dunlap. Much the richest mine of information on early American painters, sculptors, architects, engravers, miniaturists, etc. The only source of information for scores of artists, the major primary source for many others. Unabridged reprint of rare original 1834 edition, with new introduction by James T. Flexner, and 394 new illustrations. Edited by Rita Weiss. 6⅝ x 9⅝.
21695-0, 21696-9, 21697-7 Three volumes, Paperbound $15.00

EPOCHS OF CHINESE AND JAPANESE ART, Ernest F. Fenollosa. From primitive Chinese art to the 20th century, thorough history, explanation of every important art period and form, including Japanese woodcuts; main stress on China and Japan, but Tibet, Korea also included. Still unexcelled for its detailed, rich coverage of cultural background, aesthetic elements, diffusion studies, particularly of the historical period. 2nd, 1913 edition. 242 illustrations. lii + 439pp. of text.
20364-6, 20365-4 Two volumes, Paperbound $6.00

THE GENTLE ART OF MAKING ENEMIES, James A. M. Whistler. Greatest wit of his day deflates Oscar Wilde, Ruskin, Swinburne; strikes back at inane critics, exhibitions, art journalism; aesthetics of impressionist revolution in most striking form. Highly readable classic by great painter. Reproduction of edition designed by Whistler. Introduction by Alfred Werner. xxxvi + 334pp.
21875-9 Paperbound $3.00

VISUAL ILLUSIONS: THEIR CAUSES, CHARACTERISTICS, AND APPLICATIONS, Matthew Luckiesh. Thorough description and discussion of optical illusion, geometric and perspective, particularly; size and shape distortions, illusions of color, of motion; natural illusions; use of illusion in art and magic, industry, etc. Most useful today with op art, also for classical art. Scores of effects illustrated. Introduction by William H. Ittleson. 100 illustrations. xxi + 252pp.
21530-X Paperbound $2.00

A HANDBOOK OF ANATOMY FOR ART STUDENTS, Arthur Thomson. Thorough, virtually exhaustive coverage of skeletal structure, musculature, etc. Full text, supplemented by anatomical diagrams and drawings and by photographs of undraped figures. Unique in its comparison of male and female forms, pointing out differences of contour, texture, form. 211 figures, 40 drawings, 86 photographs. xx + 459pp. 5⅜ x 8⅜.
21163-0 Paperbound $3.50

150 MASTERPIECES OF DRAWING, Selected by Anthony Toney. Full page reproductions of drawings from the early 16th to the end of the 18th century, all beautifully reproduced: Rembrandt, Michelangelo, Dürer, Fragonard, Urs, Graf, Wouwerman, many others. First-rate browsing book, model book for artists. xviii + 150pp. 8⅜ x 11¼.
21032-4 Paperbound' $3.50

THE LATER WORK OF AUBREY BEARDSLEY, Aubrey Beardsley. Exotic, erotic, ironic masterpieces in full maturity: Comedy Ballet, Venus and Tannhauser, Pierrot, Lysistrata, Rape of the Lock, Savoy material, Ali Baba, Volpone, etc. This material revolutionized the art world, and is still powerful, fresh, brilliant. With *The Early Work,* all Beardsley's finest work. 174 plates, 2 in color. xiv + 176pp. 8⅛ x 11.
21817-1 Paperbound $3.75

DRAWINGS OF REMBRANDT, Rembrandt van Rijn. Complete reproduction of fabulously rare edition by Lippmann and Hofstede de Groot, completely reedited, updated, improved by Prof. Seymour Slive, Fogg Museum. Portraits, Biblical sketches, landscapes, Oriental types, nudes, episodes from classical mythology—All Rembrandt's fertile genius. Also selection of drawings by his pupils and followers. "Stunning volumes," *Saturday Review.* 550 illustrations. lxxviii + 552pp. 9⅛ x 12¼.
21485-0, 21486-9 Two volumes, Paperbound $10.00

THE DISASTERS OF WAR, Francisco Goya. One of the masterpieces of Western civilization—83 etchings that record Goya's shattering, bitter reaction to the Napoleonic war that swept through Spain after the insurrection of 1808 and to war in general. Reprint of the first edition, with three additional plates from Boston's Museum of Fine Arts. All plates facsimile size. Introduction by Philip Hofer, Fogg Museum. v + 97pp. 9⅜ x 8¼.
21872-4 Paperbound $2.50

GRAPHIC WORKS OF ODILON REDON. Largest collection of Redon's graphic works ever assembled: 172 lithographs, 28 etchings and engravings, 9 drawings. These include some of his most famous works. All the plates from *Odilon Redon: oeuvre graphique complet,* plus additional plates. New introduction and caption translations by Alfred Werner. 209 illustrations. xxvii + 209pp. 9⅛ x 12¼.
21966-8 Paperbound $5.00

DESIGN BY ACCIDENT; A BOOK OF "ACCIDENTAL EFFECTS" FOR ARTISTS AND DESIGNERS, James F. O'Brien. Create your own unique, striking, imaginative effects by "controlled accident" interaction of materials: paints and lacquers, oil and water based paints, splatter, crackling materials, shatter, similar items. Everything you do will be different; first book on this limitless art, so useful to both fine artist and commercial artist. Full instructions. 192 plates showing "accidents," 8 in color. viii + 215pp. 8⅜ x 11¼.   21942-9 Paperbound $3.75

THE BOOK OF SIGNS, Rudolf Koch. Famed German type designer draws 493 beautiful symbols: religious, mystical, alchemical, imperial, property marks, runes, etc. Remarkable fusion of traditional and modern. Good for suggestions of timelessness, smartness, modernity. Text. vi + 104pp. 6⅛ x 9¼.
20162-7 Paperbound $1.25

HISTORY OF INDIAN AND INDONESIAN ART, Ananda K. Coomaraswamy. An unabridged republication of one of the finest books by a great scholar in Eastern art. Rich in descriptive material, history, social backgrounds; Sunga reliefs, Rajput paintings, Gupta temples, Burmese frescoes, textiles, jewelry, sculpture, etc. 400 photos. viii + 423pp. 6⅜ x 9¾.   21436-2 Paperbound $5.00

PRIMITIVE ART, Franz Boas. America's foremost anthropologist surveys textiles, ceramics, woodcarving, basketry, metalwork, etc.; patterns, technology, creation of symbols, style origins. All areas of world, but very full on Northwest Coast Indians. More than 350 illustrations of baskets, boxes, totem poles, weapons, etc. 378 pp.
20025-6 Paperbound $3.00

THE GENTLEMAN AND CABINET MAKER'S DIRECTOR, Thomas Chippendale. Full reprint (third edition, 1762) of most influential furniture book of all time, by master cabinetmaker. 200 plates, illustrating chairs, sofas, mirrors, tables, cabinets, plus 24 photographs of surviving pieces. Biographical introduction by N. Bienenstock. vi + 249pp. 9⅞ x 12¾.   21601-2 Paperbound $4.00

AMERICAN ANTIQUE FURNITURE, Edgar G. Miller, Jr. The basic coverage of all American furniture before 1840. Individual chapters cover type of furniture—clocks, tables, sideboards, etc.—chronologically, with inexhaustible wealth of data. More than 2100 photographs, all identified, commented on. Essential to all early American collectors. Introduction by H. E. Keyes. vi + 1106pp. 7⅞ x 10¾.
21599-7, 21600-4 Two volumes, Paperbound $11.00

PENNSYLVANIA DUTCH AMERICAN FOLK ART, Henry J. Kauffman. 279 photos, 28 drawings of tulipware, Fraktur script, painted tinware, toys, flowered furniture, quilts, samplers, hex signs, house interiors, etc. Full descriptive text. Excellent for tourist, rewarding for designer, collector. Map. 146pp. 7⅞ x 10¾.
21205-X Paperbound $2.50

EARLY NEW ENGLAND GRAVESTONE RUBBINGS, Edmund V. Gillon, Jr. 43 photographs, 226 carefully reproduced rubbings show heavily symbolic, sometimes macabre early gravestones, up to early 19th century. Remarkable early American primitive art, occasionally strikingly beautiful; always powerful. Text. xxvi + 207pp. 8⅜ x 11¼.   21380-3 Paperbound $3.50

ALPHABETS AND ORNAMENTS, Ernst Lehner. Well-known pictorial source for decorative alphabets, script examples, cartouches, frames, decorative title pages, calligraphic initials, borders, similar material. 14th to 19th century, mostly European. Useful in almost any graphic arts designing, varied styles. 750 illustrations. 256pp. 7 x 10.   21905-4 Paperbound $4.00

PAINTING: A CREATIVE APPROACH, Norman Colquhoun. For the beginner simple guide provides an instructive approach to painting: major stumbling blocks for beginner; overcoming them, technical points; paints and pigments; oil painting; watercolor and other media and color. New section on "plastic" paints. Glossary. Formerly *Paint Your Own Pictures*. 221pp.   22000-1 Paperbound $1.75

THE ENJOYMENT AND USE OF COLOR, Walter Sargent. Explanation of the relations between colors themselves and between colors in nature and art, including hundreds of little-known facts about color values, intensities, effects of high and low illumination, complementary colors. Many practical hints for painters, references to great masters. 7 color plates, 29 illustrations. x + 274pp.
20944-X Paperbound $2.75

THE NOTEBOOKS OF LEONARDO DA VINCI, compiled and edited by Jean Paul Richter. 1566 extracts from original manuscripts reveal the full range of Leonardo's versatile genius: all his writings on painting, sculpture, architecture, anatomy, astronomy, geography, topography, physiology, mining, music, etc., in both Italian and English, with 186 plates of manuscript pages and more than 500 additional drawings. Includes studies for the Last Supper, the lost Sforza monument, and other works. Total of xlvii + 866pp. 7⅞ x 10¾.
22572-0, 22573-9 Two volumes, Paperbound $11.00

MONTGOMERY WARD CATALOGUE OF 1895. Tea gowns, yards of flannel and pillow-case lace, stereoscopes, books of gospel hymns, the New Improved Singer Sewing Machine, side saddles, milk skimmers, straight-edged razors, high-button shoes, spittoons, and on and on . . . listing some 25,000 items, practically all illustrated. Essential to the shoppers of the 1890's, it is our truest record of the spirit of the period. Unaltered reprint of Issue No. 57, Spring and Summer 1895. Introduction by Boris Emmet. Innumerable illustrations. xiii + 624pp. 8½ x 11⅝.
22377-9 Paperbound $6.95

THE CRYSTAL PALACE EXHIBITION ILLUSTRATED CATALOGUE (LONDON, 1851). One of the wonders of the modern world—the Crystal Palace Exhibition in which all the nations of the civilized world exhibited their achievements in the arts and sciences—presented in an equally important illustrated catalogue. More than 1700 items pictured with accompanying text—ceramics, textiles, cast-iron work, carpets, pianos, sleds, razors, wall-papers, billiard tables, beehives, silverware and hundreds of other artifacts—represent the focal point of Victorian culture in the Western World. Probably the largest collection of Victorian decorative art ever assembled—indispensable for antiquarians and designers. Unabridged republication of the Art-Journal Catalogue of the Great Exhibition of 1851, with all terminal essays. New introduction by John Gloag, F.S.A. xxxiv + 426pp. 9 x 12.
22503-8 Paperbound $5.00

A History of Costume, Carl Köhler. Definitive history, based on surviving pieces of clothing primarily, and paintings, statues, etc. secondarily. Highly readable text, supplemented by 594 illustrations of costumes of the ancient Mediterranean peoples, Greece and Rome, the Teutonic prehistoric period; costumes of the Middle Ages, Renaissance, Baroque, 18th and 19th centuries. Clear, measured patterns are provided for many clothing articles. Approach is practical throughout. Enlarged by Emma von Sichart. 464pp. 21030-8 Paperbound $3.50

Oriental Rugs, Antique and Modern, Walter A. Hawley. A complete and authoritative treatise on the Oriental rug—where they are made, by whom and how, designs and symbols, characteristics in detail of the six major groups, how to distinguish them and how to buy them. Detailed technical data is provided on periods, weaves, warps, wefts, textures, sides, ends and knots, although no technical background is required for an understanding. 11 color plates, 80 halftones, 4 maps. vi + 320pp. 6⅛ x 9⅛. 22366-3 Paperbound $5.00

Ten Books on Architecture, Vitruvius. By any standards the most important book on architecture ever written. Early Roman discussion of aesthetics of building, construction methods, orders, sites, and every other aspect of architecture has inspired, instructed architecture for about 2,000 years. Stands behind Palladio, Michelangelo, Bramante, Wren, countless others. Definitive Morris H. Morgan translation. 68 illustrations. xii + 331pp. 20645-9 Paperbound $3.00

The Four Books of Architecture, Andrea Palladio. Translated into every major Western European language in the two centuries following its publication in 1570, this has been one of the most influential books in the history of architecture. Complete reprint of the 1738 Isaac Ware edition. New introduction by Adolf Placzek, Columbia Univ. 216 plates. xxii + 110pp. of text. 9½ x 12¾. 21308-0 Clothbound $12.50

Sticks and Stones: A Study of American Architecture and Civilization, Lewis Mumford.One of the great classics of American cultural history. American architecture from the medieval-inspired earliest forms to the early 20th century; evolution of structure and style, and reciprocal influences on environment. 21 photographic illustrations. 238pp. 20202-X Paperbound $2.00

The American Builder's Companion, Asher Benjamin. The most widely used early 19th century architectural style and source book, for colonial up into Greek Revival periods. Extensive development of geometry of carpentering, construction of sashes, frames, doors, stairs; plans and elevations of domestic and other buildings. Hundreds of thousands of houses were built according to this book, now invaluable to historians, architects, restorers, etc. 1827 edition. 59 plates. 114pp. 7⅞ x 10¾. 22236-5 Paperbound $3.50

Dutch Houses in the Hudson Valley Before 1776, Helen Wilkinson Reynolds. The standard survey of the Dutch colonial house and outbuildings, with constructional features, decoration, and local history associated with individual homesteads. Introduction by Franklin D. Roosevelt. Map. 150 illustrations. 469pp. 6⅝ x 9¼. 21469-9 Paperbound $5.00

THE ARCHITECTURE OF COUNTRY HOUSES, Andrew J. Downing. Together with Vaux's *Villas and Cottages* this is the basic book for Hudson River Gothic architecture of the middle Victorian period. Full, sound discussions of general aspects of housing, architecture, style, decoration, furnishing, together with scores of detailed house plans, illustrations of specific buildings, accompanied by full text. Perhaps the most influential single American architectural book. 1850 edition. Introduction by J. Stewart Johnson. 321 figures, 34 architectural designs. xvi + 560pp.

22003-6 Paperbound $4.00

LOST EXAMPLES OF COLONIAL ARCHITECTURE, John Mead Howells. Full-page photographs of buildings that have disappeared or been so altered as to be denatured, including many designed by major early American architects. 245 plates. xvii + 248pp. 7⅞ x 10¾.

21143-6 Paperbound $3.50

DOMESTIC ARCHITECTURE OF THE AMERICAN COLONIES AND OF THE EARLY REPUBLIC, Fiske Kimball. Foremost architect and restorer of Williamsburg and Monticello covers nearly 200 homes between 1620-1825. Architectural details, construction, style features, special fixtures, floor plans, etc. Generally considered finest work in its area. 219 illustrations of houses, doorways, windows, capital mantels. xx + 314pp. 7⅞ x 10¾.

21743-4 Paperbound $4.00

EARLY AMERICAN ROOMS: 1650-1858, edited by Russell Hawes Kettell. Tour of 12 rooms, each representative of a different era in American history and each furnished, decorated, designed and occupied in the style of the era. 72 plans and elevations, 8-page color section, etc., show fabrics, wall papers, arrangements, etc. Full descriptive text. xvii + 200pp. of text. 8⅜ x 11¼.

21633-0 Paperbound $5.00

THE FITZWILLIAM VIRGINAL BOOK, edited by J. Fuller Maitland and W. B. Squire. Full modern printing of famous early 17th-century ms. volume of 300 works by Morley, Byrd, Bull, Gibbons, etc. For piano or other modern keyboard instrument; easy to read format. xxxvi + 938pp. 8⅜ x 11.

21068-5, 21069-3 Two volumes, Paperbound $10.00

KEYBOARD MUSIC, Johann Sebastian Bach. Bach Gesellschaft edition. A rich selection of Bach's masterpieces for the harpsichord: the six English Suites, six French Suites, the six Partitas (Clavierübung part I), the Goldberg Variations (Clavierübung part IV), the fifteen Two-Part Inventions and the fifteen Three-Part Sinfonias. Clearly reproduced on large sheets with ample margins; eminently playable. vi + 312pp. 8⅛ x 11.

22360-4 Paperbound $5.00

THE MUSIC OF BACH: AN INTRODUCTION, Charles Sanford Terry. A fine, nontechnical introduction to Bach's music, both instrumental and vocal. Covers organ music, chamber music, passion music, other types. Analyzes themes, developments, innovations. x + 114pp.

21075-8 Paperbound $1.50

BEETHOVEN AND HIS NINE SYMPHONIES, Sir George Grove. Noted British musicologist provides best history, analysis, commentary on symphonies. Very thorough, rigorously accurate; necessary to both advanced student and amateur music lover. 436 musical passages. vii + 407 pp.

20334-4 Paperbound $2.75

JOHANN SEBASTIAN BACH, Philipp Spitta. One of the great classics of musicology, this definitive analysis of Bach's music (and life) has never been surpassed. Lucid, nontechnical analyses of hundreds of pieces (30 pages devoted to St. Matthew Passion, 26 to B Minor Mass). Also includes major analysis of 18th-century music. 450 musical examples. 40-page musical supplement. Total of xx + 1799pp.
(EUK) 22278-0, 22279-9 Two volumes, Clothbound $17.50

MOZART AND HIS PIANO CONCERTOS, Cuthbert Girdlestone. The only full-length study of an important area of Mozart's creativity. Provides detailed analyses of all 23 concertos, traces inspirational sources. 417 musical examples. Second edition. 509pp. 21271-8 Paperbound $3.50

THE PERFECT WAGNERITE: A COMMENTARY ON THE NIBLUNG'S RING, George Bernard Shaw. Brilliant and still relevant criticism in remarkable essays on Wagner's Ring cycle, Shaw's ideas on political and social ideology behind the plots, role of Leitmotifs, vocal requisites, etc. Prefaces. xxi + 136pp.
(USO) 21707-8 Paperbound $1.75

DON GIOVANNI, W. A. Mozart. Complete libretto, modern English translation; biographies of composer and librettist; accounts of early performances and critical reaction. Lavishly illustrated. All the material you need to understand and appreciate this great work. Dover Opera Guide and Libretto Series; translated and introduced by Ellen Bleiler. 92 illustrations. 209pp.
21134-7 Paperbound $2.00

BASIC ELECTRICITY, U. S. Bureau of Naval Personel. Originally a training course, best non-technical coverage of basic theory of electricity and its applications. Fundamental concepts, batteries, circuits, conductors and wiring techniques, AC and DC, inductance and capacitance, generators, motors, transformers, magnetic amplifiers, synchros, servomechanisms, etc. Also covers blue-prints, electrical diagrams, etc. Many questions, with answers. 349 illustrations. x + 448pp. 6½ x 9¼.
20973-3 Paperbound $3.50

REPRODUCTION OF SOUND, Edgar Villchur. Thorough coverage for laymen of high fidelity systems, reproducing systems in general, needles, amplifiers, preamps, loudspeakers, feedback, explaining physical background. "A rare talent for making technicalities vividly comprehensible," R. Darrell, *High Fidelity*. 69 figures. iv + 92pp. 21515-6 Paperbound $1.35

HEAR ME TALKIN' TO YA: THE STORY OF JAZZ AS TOLD BY THE MEN WHO MADE IT, Nat Shapiro and Nat Hentoff. Louis Armstrong, Fats Waller, Jo Jones, Clarence Williams, Billy Holiday, Duke Ellington, Jelly Roll Morton and dozens of other jazz greats tell how it was in Chicago's South Side, New Orleans, depression Harlem and the modern West Coast as jazz was born and grew. xvi + 429pp.
21726-4 Paperbound $3.00

FABLES OF AESOP, translated by Sir Roger L'Estrange. A reproduction of the very rare 1931 Paris edition; a selection of the most interesting fables, together with 50 imaginative drawings by Alexander Calder. v + 128pp. 6½x9¼.
21780-9 Paperbound $1.50

AGAINST THE GRAIN (A REBOURS), Joris K. Huysmans. Filled with weird images, evidences of a bizarre imagination, exotic experiments with hallucinatory drugs, rich tastes and smells and the diversions of its sybarite hero Duc Jean des Esseintes, this classic novel pushed 19th-century literary decadence to its limits. Full un-abridged edition. Do not confuse this with abridged editions generally sold. Intro-duction by Havelock Ellis. xlix + 206pp. 22190-3 Paperbound $2.50

VARIORUM SHAKESPEARE: HAMLET. Edited by Horace H. Furness; a landmark of American scholarship. Exhaustive footnotes and appendices treat all doubtful words and phrases, as well as suggested critical emendations throughout the play's history. First volume contains editor's own text, collated with all Quartos and Folios. Second volume contains full first Quarto, translations of Shakespeare's sources (Belleforest, and Saxo Grammaticus), Der Bestrafte Brudermord, and many essays on critical and historical points of interest by major authorities of past and present. Includes details of staging and costuming over the years. By far the best edition available for serious students of Shakespeare. Total of xx + 905pp. 21004-9, 21005-7, 2 volumes, Paperbound $7.00

A LIFE OF WILLIAM SHAKESPEARE, Sir Sidney Lee. This is the standard life of Shakespeare, summarizing everything known about Shakespeare and his plays. Incredibly rich in material, broad in coverage, clear and judicious, it has served thousands as the best introduction to Shakespeare. 1931 edition. 9 plates. xxix + 792pp. 21967-4 Paperbound $4.50

MASTERS OF THE DRAMA, John Gassner. Most comprehensive history of the drama in print, covering every tradition from Greeks to modern Europe and America, including India, Far East, etc. Covers more than 800 dramatists, 2000 plays, with biographical material, plot summaries, theatre history, criticism, etc. "Best of its kind in English," New Republic. 77 illustrations. xxii + 890pp. 20100-7 Clothbound $10.00

THE EVOLUTION OF THE ENGLISH LANGUAGE, George McKnight. The growth of English, from the 14th century to the present. Unusual, non-technical account presents basic information in very interesting form: sound shifts, change in grammar and syntax, vocabulary growth, similar topics. Abundantly illustrated with quota-tions. Formerly Modern English in the Making. xii + 590pp. 21932-1 Paperbound $4.00

AN ETYMOLOGICAL DICTIONARY OF MODERN ENGLISH, Ernest Weekley. Fullest, richest work of its sort, by foremost British lexicographer. Detailed word histories, including many colloquial and archaic words; extensive quotations. Do not con-fuse this with the Concise Etymological Dictionary, which is much abridged. Total of xxvii + 830pp. 6½ x 9¼. 21873-2, 21874-0 Two volumes, Paperbound $7.90

FLATLAND: A ROMANCE OF MANY DIMENSIONS, E. A. Abbott. Classic of science-fiction explores ramifications of life in a two-dimensional world, and what happens when a three-dimensional being intrudes. Amusing reading, but also use-ful as introduction to thought about hyperspace. Introduction by Banesh Hoffmann. 16 illustrations. xx + 103pp. 20001-9 Paperbound $1.25

POEMS OF ANNE BRADSTREET, edited with an introduction by Robert Hutchinson. A new selection of poems by America's first poet and perhaps the first significant woman poet in the English language. 48 poems display her development in works of considerable variety—love poems, domestic poems, religious meditations, formal elegies, "quaternions," etc. Notes, bibliography. viii + 222pp.
22160-1 Paperbound $2.50

THREE GOTHIC NOVELS: THE CASTLE OF OTRANTO BY HORACE WALPOLE; VATHEK BY WILLIAM BECKFORD; THE VAMPYRE BY JOHN POLIDORI, WITH FRAGMENT OF A NOVEL BY LORD BYRON, edited by E. F. Bleiler. The first Gothic novel, by Walpole; the finest Oriental tale in English, by Beckford; powerful Romantic supernatural story in versions by Polidori and Byron. All extremely important in history of literature; all still exciting, packed with supernatural thrills, ghosts, haunted castles, magic, etc. xl + 291pp.
21232-7 Paperbound $2.50

THE BEST TALES OF HOFFMANN, E. T. A. Hoffmann. 10 of Hoffmann's most important stories, in modern re-editings of standard translations: Nutcracker and the King of Mice, Signor Formica, Automata, The Sandman, Rath Krespel, The Golden Flowerpot, Master Martin the Cooper, The Mines of Falun, The King's Betrothed, A New Year's Eve Adventure. 7 illustrations by Hoffmann. Edited by E. F. Bleiler. xxxix + 419pp.   21793-0 Paperbound $3.00

GHOST AND HORROR STORIES OF AMBROSE BIERCE, Ambrose Bierce. 23 strikingly modern stories of the horrors latent in the human mind: The Eyes of the Panther, The Damned Thing, An Occurrence at Owl Creek Bridge, An Inhabitant of Carcosa, etc., plus the dream-essay, Visions of the Night. Edited by E. F. Bleiler. xxii + 199pp.   20767-6 Paperbound $1.50

BEST GHOST STORIES OF J. S. LeFANU, J. Sheridan LeFanu. Finest stories by Victorian master often considered greatest supernatural writer of all. Carmilla, Green Tea, The Haunted Baronet, The Familiar, and 12 others. Most never before available in the U. S. A. Edited by E. F. Bleiler. 8 illustrations from Victorian publications. xvii + 467pp.   20415-4 Paperbound $3.00

MATHEMATICAL FOUNDATIONS OF INFORMATION THEORY, A. I. Khinchin. Comprehensive introduction to work of Shannon, McMillan, Feinstein and Khinchin, placing these investigations on a rigorous mathematical basis. Covers entropy concept in probability theory, uniqueness theorem, Shannon's inequality, ergodic sources, the E property, martingale concept, noise, Feinstein's fundamental lemma, Shanon's first and second theorems. Translated by R. A. Silverman and M. D. Friedman. iii + 120pp.   60434-9 Paperbound $2.00

SEVEN SCIENCE FICTION NOVELS, H. G. Wells. The standard collection of the great novels. Complete, unabridged. *First Men in the Moon, Island of Dr. Moreau, War of the Worlds, Food of the Gods, Invisible Man, Time Machine, In the Days of the Comet.* Not only science fiction fans, but every educated person owes it to himself to read these novels. 1015pp.   (USO) 20264-X Clothbound $6.00

LAST AND FIRST MEN AND STAR MAKER, TWO SCIENCE FICTION NOVELS, Olaf Stapledon. Greatest future histories in science fiction. In the first, human intelligence is the "hero," through strange paths of evolution, interplanetary invasions, incredible technologies, near extinctions and reemergences. Star Maker describes the quest of a band of star rovers for intelligence itself, through time and space: weird inhuman civilizations, crustacean minds, symbiotic worlds, etc. Complete, unabridged. v + 438pp. (USO) 21962-3 Paperbound $2.50

THREE PROPHETIC NOVELS, H. G. WELLS. Stages of a consistently planned future for mankind. *When the Sleeper Wakes,* and *A Story of the Days to Come,* anticipate *Brave New World* and *1984,* in the 21st Century; *The Time Machine,* only complete version in print, shows farther future and the end of mankind. All show Wells's greatest gifts as storyteller and novelist. Edited by E. F. Bleiler. x + 335pp. (USO) 20605-X Paperbound $2.50

THE DEVIL'S DICTIONARY, Ambrose Bierce. America's own Oscar Wilde—Ambrose Bierce—offers his barbed iconoclastic wisdom in over 1,000 definitions hailed by H. L. Mencken as "some of the most gorgeous witticisms in the English language." 145pp. 20487-1 Paperbound $1.25

MAX AND MORITZ, Wilhelm Busch. Great children's classic, father of comic strip, of two bad boys, Max and Moritz. Also Ker and Plunk (Plisch und Plumm), Cat and Mouse, Deceitful Henry, Ice-Peter, The Boy and the Pipe, and five other pieces. Original German, with English translation. Edited by H. Arthur Klein; translations by various hands and H. Arthur Klein. vi + 216pp. 20181-3 Paperbound $2.00

PIGS IS PIGS AND OTHER FAVORITES, Ellis Parker Butler. The title story is one of the best humor short stories, as Mike Flannery obfuscates biology and English. Also included, That Pup of Murchison's, The Great American Pie Company, and Perkins of Portland. 14 illustrations. v + 109pp. 21532-6 Paperbound $1.25

THE PETERKIN PAPERS, Lucretia P. Hale. It takes genius to be as stupidly mad as the Peterkins, as they decide to become wise, celebrate the "Fourth," keep a cow, and otherwise strain the resources of the Lady from Philadelphia. Basic book of American humor. 153 illustrations. 219pp. 20794-3 Paperbound $2.00

PERRAULT'S FAIRY TALES, translated by A. E. Johnson and S. R. Littlewood, with 34 full-page illustrations by Gustave Doré. All the original Perrault stories—Cinderella, Sleeping Beauty, Bluebeard, Little Red Riding Hood, Puss in Boots, Tom Thumb, etc.—with their witty verse morals and the magnificent illustrations of Doré. One of the five or six great books of European fairy tales. viii + 117pp. 8⅛ x 11. 22311-6 Paperbound $2.00

OLD HUNGARIAN FAIRY TALES, Baroness Orczy. Favorites translated and adapted by author of the *Scarlet Pimpernel.* Eight fairy tales include "The Suitors of Princess Fire-Fly," "The Twin Hunchbacks," "Mr. Cuttlefish's Love Story," and "The Enchanted Cat." This little volume of magic and adventure will captivate children as it has for generations. 90 drawings by Montagu Barstow. 96pp. (USO) 22293-4 Paperbound $1.95

The Red Fairy Book, Andrew Lang. Lang's color fairy books have long been children's favorites. This volume includes Rapunzel, Jack and the Bean-stalk and 35 other stories, familiar and unfamiliar. 4 plates, 93 illustrations x + 367pp.
21673-X Paperbound $2.50

The Blue Fairy Book, Andrew Lang. Lang's tales come from all countries and all times. Here are 37 tales from Grimm, the Arabian Nights, Greek Mythology, and other fascinating sources. 8 plates, 130 illustrations. xi + 390pp.
21437-0 Paperbound $2.75

Household Stories by the Brothers Grimm. Classic English-language edition of the well-known tales — Rumpelstiltskin, Snow White, Hansel and Gretel, The Twelve Brothers, Faithful John, Rapunzel, Tom Thumb (52 stories in all). Translated into simple, straightforward English by Lucy Crane. Ornamented with head-pieces, vignettes, elaborate decorative initials and a dozen full-page illustrations by Walter Crane. x + 269pp.
21080-4 Paperbound **$2.00**

The Merry Adventures of Robin Hood, Howard Pyle. The finest modern versions of the traditional ballads and tales about the great English outlaw. Howard Pyle's complete prose version, with every word, every illustration of the first edition. Do not confuse this facsimile of the original (1883) with modern editions that change text or illustrations. 23 plates plus many page decorations. xxii + 296pp.
22043-5 Paperbound $2.75

The Story of King Arthur and His Knights, Howard Pyle. The finest children's version of the life of King Arthur; brilliantly retold by Pyle, with 48 of his most imaginative illustrations. xviii + 313pp. 6⅛ x 9¼.
21445-1 Paperbound $2.50

The Wonderful Wizard of Oz, L. Frank Baum. America's finest children's book in facsimile of first edition with all Denslow illustrations in full color. The edition a child should have. Introduction by Martin Gardner. 23 color plates, scores of drawings. iv + 267pp.
20691-2 Paperbound $2.50

The Marvelous Land of Oz, L. Frank Baum. The second Oz book, every bit as imaginative as the Wizard. The hero is a boy named Tip, but the Scarecrow and the Tin Woodman are back, as is the Oz magic. 16 color plates, 120 drawings by John R. Neill. 287pp.
20692-0 Paperbound $2.50

The Magical Monarch of Mo, L. Frank Baum. Remarkable adventures in a land even stranger than Oz. The best of Baum's books not in the Oz series. 15 color plates and dozens of drawings by Frank Verbeck. xviii + 237pp.
21892-9 Paperbound $2.25

The Bad Child's Book of Beasts, More Beasts for Worse Children, A Moral Alphabet, Hilaire Belloc. Three complete humor classics in one volume. Be kind to the frog, and do not call him names . . . and 28 other whimsical animals. Familiar favorites and some not so well known. Illustrated by Basil Blackwell. 156pp.
(USO) 20749-8 Paperbound $1.50

EAST O' THE SUN AND WEST O' THE MOON, George W. Dasent. Considered the best of all translations of these Norwegian folk tales, this collection has been enjoyed by generations of children (and folklorists too). Includes True and Untrue, Why the Sea is Salt, East O' the Sun and West O' the Moon, Why the Bear is Stumpy-Tailed, Boots and the Troll, The Cock and the Hen, Rich Peter the Pedlar, and 52 more. The only edition with all 59 tales. 77 illustrations by Erik Werenskiold and Theodor Kittelsen. xv + 418pp. 22521-6 Paperbound $3.50

GOOPS AND HOW TO BE THEM, Gelett Burgess. Classic of tongue-in-cheek humor, masquerading as etiquette book. 87 verses, twice as many cartoons, show mischievous Goops as they demonstrate to children virtues of table manners, neatness, courtesy, etc. Favorite for generations. viii + 88pp. 6½ x 9¼. 22233-0 Paperbound $1.50

ALICE'S ADVENTURES UNDER GROUND, Lewis Carroll. The first version, quite different from the final Alice in Wonderland, printed out by Carroll himself with his own illustrations. Complete facsimile of the "million dollar" manuscript Carroll gave to Alice Liddell in 1864. Introduction by Martin Gardner. viii + 96pp. Title and dedication pages in color. 21482-6 Paperbound $1.25

THE BROWNIES, THEIR BOOK, Palmer Cox. Small as mice, cunning as foxes, exuberant and full of mischief, the Brownies go to the zoo, toy shop, seashore, circus, etc., in 24 verse adventures and 266 illustrations. Long a favorite, since their first appearance in St. Nicholas Magazine. xi + 144pp. 6⅝ x 9¼. 21265-3 Paperbound $1.75

SONGS OF CHILDHOOD, Walter De La Mare. Published (under the pseudonym Walter Ramal) when De La Mare was only 29, this charming collection has long been a favorite children's book. A facsimile of the first edition in paper, the 47 poems capture the simplicity of the nursery rhyme and the ballad, including such lyrics as I Met Eve, Tartary, The Silver Penny. vii + 106pp. (USO) 21972-0 Paperbound $2.00

THE COMPLETE NONSENSE OF EDWARD LEAR, Edward Lear. The finest 19th-century humorist-cartoonist in full: all nonsense limericks, zany alphabets, Owl and Pussycat, songs, nonsense botany, and more than 500 illustrations by Lear himself. Edited by Holbrook Jackson. xxix + 287pp. (USO) 20167-8 Paperbound $2.00

BILLY WHISKERS: THE AUTOBIOGRAPHY OF A GOAT, Frances Trego Montgomery. A favorite of children since the early 20th century, here are the escapades of that rambunctious, irresistible and mischievous goat—Billy Whiskers. Much in the spirit of Peck's Bad Boy, this is a book that children never tire of reading or hearing. All the original familiar illustrations by W. H. Fry are included: 6 color plates, 18 black and white drawings. 159pp. 22345-0 Paperbound $2.00

MOTHER GOOSE MELODIES. Faithful republication of the fabulously rare Munroe and Francis "copyright 1833" Boston edition—the most important Mother Goose collection, usually referred to as the "original." Familiar rhymes plus many rare ones, with wonderful old woodcut illustrations. Edited by E. F. Bleiler. 128pp. 4½ x 6⅜. 22577-1 Paperbound $1.00

TWO LITTLE SAVAGES; BEING THE ADVENTURES OF TWO BOYS WHO LIVED AS INDIANS AND WHAT THEY LEARNED, Ernest Thompson Seton. Great classic of nature and boyhood provides a vast range of woodlore in most palatable form, a genuinely entertaining story. Two farm boys build a teepee in woods and live in it for a month, working out Indian solutions to living problems, star lore, birds and animals, plants, etc. 293 illustrations. vii + 286pp.
20985-7 Paperbound $2.50

PETER PIPER'S PRACTICAL PRINCIPLES OF PLAIN & PERFECT PRONUNCIATION. Alliterative jingles and tongue-twisters of surprising charm, that made their first appearance in America about 1830. Republished in full with the spirited woodcut illustrations from this earliest American edition. 32pp. $4\frac{1}{2}$ x $6\frac{3}{8}$.
22560-7 Paperbound $1.00

SCIENCE EXPERIMENTS AND AMUSEMENTS FOR CHILDREN, Charles Vivian. 73 easy experiments, requiring only materials found at home or easily available, such as candles, coins, steel wool, etc.; illustrate basic phenomena like vacuum, simple chemical reaction, etc. All safe. Modern, well-planned. Formerly *Science Games for Children*. 102 photos, numerous drawings. 96pp. $6\frac{1}{8}$ x $9\frac{1}{4}$.
21856-2 Paperbound $1.25

AN INTRODUCTION TO CHESS MOVES AND TACTICS SIMPLY EXPLAINED, Leonard Barden. Informal intermediate introduction, quite strong in explaining reasons for moves. Covers basic material, tactics, important openings, traps, positional play in middle game, end game. Attempts to isolate patterns and recurrent configurations. Formerly *Chess*. 58 figures. 102pp. (USO) 21210-6 Paperbound $1.25

LASKER'S MANUAL OF CHESS, Dr. Emanuel Lasker. Lasker was not only one of the five great World Champions, he was also one of the ablest expositors, theorists, and analysts. In many ways, his Manual, permeated with his philosophy of battle, filled with keen insights, is one of the greatest works ever written on chess. Filled with analyzed games by the great players. A single-volume library that will profit almost any chess player, beginner or master. 308 diagrams. xli x 349pp.
20640-8 Paperbound $2.75

THE MASTER BOOK OF MATHEMATICAL RECREATIONS, Fred Schuh. In opinion of many the finest work ever prepared on mathematical puzzles, stunts, recreations; exhaustively thorough explanations of mathematics involved, analysis of effects, citation of puzzles and games. Mathematics involved is elementary. Translated bv F. Göbel. 194 figures. xxiv + 430pp.
22134-2 Paperbound $3.50

MATHEMATICS, MAGIC AND MYSTERY, Martin Gardner. Puzzle editor for Scientific American explains mathematics behind various mystifying tricks: card tricks, stage "mind reading," coin and match tricks, counting out games, geometric dissections, etc. Probability sets, theory of numbers clearly explained. Also provides more than 400 tricks, guaranteed to work, that you can do. 135 illustrations. xii + 176pp.
20335-2 Paperbound $1.75

MATHEMATICAL PUZZLES FOR BEGINNERS AND ENTHUSIASTS, Geoffrey Mott-Smith. 189 puzzles from easy to difficult—involving arithmetic, logic, algebra, properties of digits, probability, etc.—for enjoyment and mental stimulus. Explanation of mathematical principles behind the puzzles. 135 illustrations. viii + 248pp.
20198-8 Paperbound $1.75

PAPER FOLDING FOR BEGINNERS, William D. Murray and Francis J. Rigney. Easiest book on the market, clearest instructions on making interesting, beautiful origami. Sail boats, cups, roosters, frogs that move legs, bonbon boxes, standing birds, etc. 40 projects; more than 275 diagrams and photographs. 94pp.
20713-7 Paperbound $1.00

TRICKS AND GAMES ON THE POOL TABLE, Fred Herrmann. 79 tricks and games—some solitaires, some for two or more players, some competitive games—to entertain you between formal games. Mystifying shots and throws, unusual caroms, tricks involving such props as cork, coins, a hat, etc. Formerly *Fun on the Pool Table*. 77 figures. 95pp.
21814-7 Paperbound $1.25

HAND SHADOWS TO BE THROWN UPON THE WALL: A SERIES OF NOVEL AND AMUSING FIGURES FORMED BY THE HAND, Henry Bursill. Delightful picturebook from great-grandfather's day shows how to make 18 different hand shadows: a bird that flies, duck that quacks, dog that wags his tail, camel, goose, deer, boy, turtle, etc. Only book of its sort. vi + 33pp. 6½ x 9¼. 21779-5 Paperbound $1.00

WHITTLING AND WOODCARVING, E. J. Tangerman. 18th printing of best book on market. "If you can cut a potato you can carve" toys and puzzles, chains, chessmen, caricatures, masks, frames, woodcut blocks, surface patterns, much more. Information on tools, woods, techniques. Also goes into serious wood sculpture from Middle Ages to present, East and West. 464 photos, figures. x + 293pp.
20965-2 Paperbound $2.00

HISTORY OF PHILOSOPHY, Julián Marias. Possibly the clearest, most easily followed, best planned, most useful one-volume history of philosophy on the market; neither skimpy nor overfull. Full details on system of every major philosopher and dozens of less important thinkers from pre-Socratics up to Existentialism and later. Strong on many European figures usually omitted. Has gone through dozens of editions in Europe. 1966 edition, translated by Stanley Appelbaum and Clarence Strowbridge. xviii + 505pp.
21739-6 Paperbound $3.50

YOGA: A SCIENTIFIC EVALUATION, Kovoor T. Behanan. Scientific but non-technical study of physiological results of yoga exercises; done under auspices of Yale U. Relations to Indian thought, to psychoanalysis, etc. 16 photos. xxiii + 270pp.
20505-3 Paperbound $2.50

Prices subject to change without notice.
Available at your book dealer or write for free catalogue to Dept. GI, Dover Publications, Inc., 180 Varick St., N. Y., N. Y. 10014. Dover publishes more than 150 books each year on science, elementary and advanced mathematics, biology, music, art, literary history, social sciences and other areas.